MURDER

IN NORTH AMERICA

MURDER
IN NORTH AMERICA

Lionel Martinez

THE WELLFLEET PRESS

Publishing Director: Frank Oppel
Editorial, Design & Typography: Tony Meisel, AM Publishing Services
Origination: Regent Publishing Services Limited
Printing: Impresora Donneco International, S.A. de C.V.

Manufactured in Mexico
ISBN: 1-55521-703-6

Contents

To Joe Stamps who helped me find some of these stories, to Barbara for the usual stuff, to Joe and Calamity, my furry companions, who dream of murdering lots of mice, to Tony Meisel who dreamt of getting the manuscript on time, to Judi for all the cookies and to all those others, who in the spring and summer of 1990, sat around our dinner table commenting how horrible these stories were, and clamored for more.

Introduction

Whodunnit' and why is the standard question asked in all mystery fiction. But truth is always stranger than fiction and that may be one of the reasons why people from different backgrounds and experiences find real life murders so fascinating.

At first glance an interest in murder seems quite macabre, but for centuries the news media of almost all societies found murder a topic fit for the front pages of the daily newspapers.

Murder is a public event. If an unknown person dies, he or she may have their names mentioned for a day in the obituary column of a daily newspaper. If the person was prominent, then he or she might have a feature article on their life appear in the same newspaper. But if that person is a murder victim, the society's system of justice and the news media become involved in every aspect of that person's past. Friends and relatives of the victim have their private grief and anguish revealed to the public in print and on television. All this attention is focused on the question who did it and why.

To some, murder can be seen as the ultimate, if not final, method of conflict resolution. Simply put, the murderer is attempting to resolve some real or psychological conflict by blotting out the perceived source of the problem. To others, the mind of the murderer is different from the rest of the non-homicidal population. Through a twist of fate or some long hidden trauma, the murderer's soul developed without some vital part the rest of us share. The odd truth is that, until they murder, most killers seem to be ordinary people. No one trait sets them apart from their neighbors. No one suspects their dark secrets. Then one day the murderers are caught and they become objects that the rest of society stares at wondering what went wrong. Could the same thing happen to me?

Perhaps it is the why, after the who is found, that holds key to our fascination with murder. But even this isn't quite true, some of the most enduring murders have no conclusive endings. Jack the Ripper is a good example. This fiend has stirred up a storm of speculation as to his identity as well as his motives for over a hundred years. We are no closer now to solving this mystery than we are to finding out why a tiny fraction of people murder and the majority do not.

In this book I have brought together a broad range of murders, with differing motives, for the reader to ponder. These acts of mayhem and violence span 150 years of North American history. Murder is still murder whether was committed in 1843 or 1988. Somewhere in these pages the reader may find a common thread that links these murders together and supplies some important clue as to why. However, it is entirely possible that one might read this book strictly for fun.

Lionel Martinez
New York

1843
Murder and a
Footnote to History

By the standards of the 20th century, 1843 was not an extraordinary year. John Tyler moved into the White House as the first vice president to become president upon the death of his predecessor, William Henry Harrison. Tyler was not well liked. He was known as "Old Veto" for vetoing more than nine bills during his term of office, more than any president before him. On January 10 he successfully beat back an attempt in the House of Representatives to impeach him for gross usurpation of power.

The year was 1843. Expansionist pressures were building. The American frontier was a loose and unofficial line running along the northern state boundaries of Missouri and Illinois, and along the western state boundaries of Missouri, Arkansas and Louisiana. The line also cut into a small eastern piece of the Independent Republic of Texas. Although it was an imaginary line it had political significance in terms of the slavery issue. Politically the frontier marked the eastern edge of civilization, the relative safe areas open to settlement. West of the line lay the wild unsettled lands, lands which did not yet belong to the United States. This territory was noted on contemporary maps as including the Unorganized or Indian Territories and Northern Mexico. In a few years the expansionist pressures would result in the Mexican American War. As a result of the American victory Northern Mexico would be ceded to the United States. Included in the Mexican cession were the future states of California, New Mexico, Arizona, Utah and Nevada. The Unorganized or Indian Territories were a different matter. They already belonged to the United States since the Louisiana Purchase.

The areas that play an integral role in this tale of historical murder are Missouri and the future states of New Mexico and Kansas. Kansas was an arid and desolate place, considered useless for any agricultural endeavors. Grain farming wouldn't begin until 1874 when the Mennonites arrived in Kansas, bringing with them trunks loaded with seeds of Turkey Red. It was this strain of wheat that became the basis for the abundant crops from which the Kansas economy would later benefit.

New Mexico saw thousands of years of peaceful agricultural settlement by Native Americans, and hundreds of years of aggressive settlement by the nomadic Navajo and Apache tribes. The first Europeans arrived as a treasure seeking expedition lead by Francisco Vázquez de Coronado in the 16th century. The territory was quickly claimed by Spain and in 1610 Santa Fe became its first permanent settlement. Throughout the 17th century missionary work was the predominant activity of the area. Trade with New Mexico's next door neighbor, the United States, began in 1821 when the region became part of the Independent Republic of Mexico. The main artery of this commercial activity was Santa Fe Trail, which opened the same year. For the Missouri border towns the Santa Fe Trail and its trade link with the greater Mexican Republic meant economic survival and in some cases outright prosperity.

Missouri was named for an extinct Indian tribe whose last action was losing a battle with the Osage in 1805, thereafter the tribe dispersed and ceased to exist. The state's first white settlers were French lead miners and fur trappers. It was these intrepid Frenchmen who founded St. Louis in 1764. In 1803 Missouri became a United States possession as part of the Louisiana Purchase. The state did not see its first wave of American settlers until after the War of 1812. After much wrangling about its status Missouri entered the Union in 1821 as a slave state under the Missouri Compromise of 1820.

From the very beginning trade was important to the economy of the frontier state. Its economic lifeline was the Santa Fe Trail opened by trader William Becknell. From the Missouri River, the trail followed the divide between the tributaries of the Kansas and Arkansas rivers to somewhere near the present town of Great Bend, Kansas. At this point the trail followed the Arkansas until it separated into three routes. The shortest of these went to Santa Fe.

M.B. LAMAR,

OF TEXAS.

Mirabeau Lamar was the first president of Texas when it was a small republic. His mistakes in office set the stage for Don Antonio José Chávez's murder.

The westward flow of manufactured goods and the eastward flow of gold, silver and fur was beneficial to both partners. Silver pesos and gold doubloons from Santa Fe stabilized the rural Missouri economy. In 1839 the Bank of Missouri, one of the soundest state banks in the nation, avoided collapse by the timely deposit of $45,000 in silver brought to Missouri by an American merchant train arriving from New Mexico. The Mexicans not only gained manufactured goods at reasonable prices, but also the business of refitting the wagon trains with spare parts and the sale of grain to nourish the animals. Both Missouri and New Mexican gunsmiths, carpenters, blacksmiths and other craftsmen benefited from this arrangement. It really was quite ideal and no one wanted it to change.

Yet there were some changes during the short history of the arrangement. Early in the commercial venture most of the traders were from Missouri. But as with any good money-making idea, everyone wanted to get in on the act., especially the old aristocratic families of New Mexico. Mexican trade grew and for these aristocratic families commerce flourished after a small successful overture to the U.S. government, in 1826, asking permission to allow Mexican merchants to trade directly across open borders. By 1843 the majority of the Santa Fe Trail traders were Mexican. No one at either end of the trail complained. Everyone remotely involved in the Santa Fe commerce was making a profit from the trade.

Unlike our crime-ridden times, when government officials, financiers, stock brokers and bank presidents seem to vie with one another to see how much money they can steal, there was very little lawlessness at that time in either Santa Fe or Independence, the American and Mexican terminuses of the Santa Fe Trail. It was not unknown for goods shipped from St. Louis to stand unguarded in Independence for weeks until they were ready for shipment to Santa Fe. Once a member of the Chávez Mexican merchant family left $100,000 in silver coins outside a store where he was going to conduct his business the next day. Not one coin was missing in the morning. Trust was so great on that part of the frontier, banks would lend unsecured loans for a year confident that they would be paid back.

During this time living legends actually traveled the Santa Fe Trail. Giants such as Kit Carson, Daniel Boone, Davy Crockett and John C. Frémont were common visitors to both Missouri and New Mexico.

It was also a time when omens, either supernatural or religious, appeared and were taken seriously. Comets scarred the heavens, floods scoured the country, rumors of a new locust plague flew through the farmlands and the end of the world was seen to be just around the corner. In New York state, William Miller, a farmer by occupation and a converted Baptist by inclination, preached for almost 10 years that Christ would return on March 21, 1843. With his talk of impending Judgment Day, he gained a few thousand followers. When Miller's end of the world did not arrive on schedule, he admitted to a small miscalculation and set another date.

Into this time of settled trade and unsettling omens a murderous passion was released, and it came from the direction of the Independent Republic of Texas. Upon winning the battle of San Jacinto in 1836, and since its independence from Mexico, Texas looked to conquering the province of New Mexico. In 1841, Mirabeau Lamar, president of the small republic, sent an expedition of over 300 men to Santa Fe to achieve this goal. Lamar reasoned that even if the campaign failed to assert Texas' claim to the land, it would surely wrench away a sizable portion of the profitable Santa Fe trade for the financially strapped republic. The soldiers lost their way and the invasion was a disaster. When they arrived at the eastern settlements of New Mexico the expedition was nearly starving and their morale was nonexistent. With very little effort the Mexican army easily defeated the ragged Texans and the winners marched the surviving invaders off to prison in Mexico City. Enter the U.S. government. After several weeks of heated diplomatic negotiations the prisoners were released.

Later the same year Sam Houston defeated Lamar's bid for a second term. The new president faced the same economic problems as his predecessor— the treasury was on the brink of collapse. It had been chronically short of cash under Lamar. Texas had met with limited success seeking loans from European governments. Two years later the new republic still needed funds. Houston began to think of how he could expand trade. His solutions were the same as his predecessor's. Either Texas should annex from Northern Mexico or divert some of the traffic on the Santa Fe Trail towards Texas. The following year began with an interesting proposition.

Charles Alexander Warfield was the well educated son of a New Orleans merchant and a bit of an adventurer. He had traveled the Southwest in search of new experiences and new enterprises, and was intimately knowledgeable of the commerce along the Santa Fe Trail. With the help of some of his New Orleans contacts Warfield offered his services to President Houston. It was a package deal. The young man proposed to win the hearts and minds of the New Mexicans for Texas. His strategy was simple; he would lead an expedition of volunteers on a takeover of the government of New Mexico. In return Warfield wanted half of all booty seized, the remaining half would fill the Texas treasury. There was nothing wrong with his plan, except it sounded suspiciously like the failed expedition of "41."

Warfield added a new wrinkle to the scheme. He wanted the plan to be kept secret. Only a few individuals at the highest levels of government were to know about his mission. Warfield would pose as a mercenary raider and not as an agent in the employ of the Texas government. This cover would enable him to enlist anywhere between 500 and 1,000 hand-picked men of his choosing, and he would not have to worry about recruits who might have divided loyalties between Warfield's cause and their other beliefs. At the same time he wanted a letter of authority stating that he was working for Texas along with a commission as colonel. The letter of authority was to insure that Northern Mexico could legally be annexed by Texas after Warfield and his band conquered it. The commission as colonel was for his ego and to give him the military authority to carry out his mission.

Sam Houston was delighted. This opportunity could not have come at a better time. Since the 1841 unsuccessful raid in New Mexico, the Mexicans had become quite testy. They had carried out a series of small raids culminating in the temporary seizing of San Antonio. In all cases the Mexicans were beaten back to their own land. The new president wanted to show that Texas was not to be taken lightly, and he wanted revenge.

Warfield's notion seemed to solve the need for revenge and provide a solution to the economic crisis with one bold stroke. So Houston ordered the secretary of war, George W. Hockley, to obtain the authorization for Warfield's invasion of New Mexico.

Hockley took the subject of secrecy very seriously; he told no one in the Texas government or Congress about the plan. He obtained the requested documents and commission. The wagon wheel of fate was ready to turn in some unexpected ways.

Armed with the proper authorization and colonel's rank, Warfield began the task of recruiting his army. He started in Texas, traveled through Arkansas and sometime in October 1842 he ended up in St. Louis, Missouri. For someone who wanted to keep his real mission shrouded in secrecy the colonel was quite the carnival barker. He immediately attracted everyone's notice by promising rich rewards and officer's commissions in the Texas army. As if to underscore the last inducement, Warfield was seen on a number of occasions brandishing blank commissions in the Texas military service. It is unknown, but doubtful, whether he signed up any recruits in Saint Louis.

His next stop was across the state, to the imaginary frontier line, in Independence. Here he found men willing to undertake his enterprise. Two of them were brothers, John and David McDaniel from the town of Liberty. Liberty was only 10 miles away from Independence and on the other side of the Missouri River, but as far as knowing who was who and what was what.... All the townsfolk of Independence knew about the McDaniels was that they came from good family. John could be a very charming man when he needed to be. No one at the time knew that John had become an outlaw and killer after serving in the Texas militia a few years before. No one in the 1840s could have diagnosed that John had what in modern times is called a sociopathic personality. Later people would say his moral character was badly flawed.

Warfield signed up close to 60 men at Independence. He was so impressed by John McDaniel's charm that he used one of his much brandished blank commissions to make McDaniel a captain in the Texas military. The colonel also put John in charge of his new recruits and asked him to find more. Warfield straight away set out toward the Rocky Mountains to enroll more members for his merry band of adventurers.

John McDaniel was left specific instructions as to when and where to join Col. Warfield. He was also given the gist of the invasion plans of New Mexico. On May 15, Warfield, and his newly enlisted men from the Rocky Mountains, would meet McDaniel and his detachment at Point of Rocks on the Santa Fe Trail. Point of Rocks was close to the edge the Mexican border. On the same day a small contingent of Texas enrollees was expected to arrive at the meeting place. Once joined, this paramilitary outfit would ravage the trail, taking Mexican plunder wherever it could be found. As soon as they had cleared the trade route, they would travel due southwest and begin their glorious invasion of Mexico.

The plan was bold. It was audacious. It began to unravel as soon as Warfield left Independence.

McDaniel had five months to kill before he was due to meet Warfield at Point of Rocks. He had nothing but time on his hands and he spent that time at Yoacham's Tavern in nearby Westport, Missouri. Capt. John McDaniel did recruit some more men for the cause. He also lost most of the men that Warfield had enlisted. Within a relatively short time the nature of the Missouri company changed from earnest young men seeking fame, fortune and glory to a gang of land pirates. Much of this transformation can be attributed to John McDaniel's lack of

Sam Houston, Texas' second president, thought the only way out of his predecessor's mess was to annex Northern Mexico and divert some of the commercial traffic on the Santa Fe Trail toward Texas. Underneath it all Houston wanted to show that Texas was not to be taken lightly. He believed Warfield's plan could easily accomplish these goals. Houston got more than he bargained for.

leadership qualities and apathy for any patriotic crusade. The other reason for this shift of focus was the newly appointed captain's true interest, plunder. By Christmas McDaniel was the leader of 14 desperate men who relished the rather novel idea that their criminal enterprise enjoyed the legitimate cover of a Texas military commission.

It has been suggested by historians that sometime during the months spent plotting and drinking at Yoacham's Tavern the group learned a Mexican trader, Don Antonio José Chávez, was due in Missouri the following spring, and he would be traveling along the Santa Fe Trail. It was widely known that the Chávez caravans carried a considerable amount of silver coins during their trading expeditions. In 1840 Antonio José and his brothers had carried over $60,000 in silver along the Santa Fe Trail into Missouri.

The youngest of the brothers, Antonio José Chávez, was a member of a long established and prosperous Mexican family. They had been involved in Mexican government and trade since 1598 and by 1843 their commercial empire included large tracts of land with considerable investments in livestock and other businesses. The Chávez family was closely linked by a series of marriages to several other prominent families of the province. After Mexico became independent from Spain, Antonio's father was the first governor of New Mexico. Keeping with the newly founded political tradition, his oldest brother, Mariano, became the president of the New Mexican provincial assembly and in 1844 he would become the acting governor of New Mexico.

In a typical trading year the search for advantageous prices might send the Chávezes traveling further and further eastward. Their first stops in the United States were Independence and Westport. Both places offered merchandise at wholesale prices, but often the selection was limited and far more costly than might be found further east. From Independence one or more of the Chávezes would take a steamboat to St. Louis. On an off year even this trading center might not offer a wide enough selection at the right price. That would mean a trip by steamboat, railroad and stagecoach to the great Eastern cities of Pittsburgh and New York.

While they were away on the trip to the East their crews, animals and wagons would patiently wait in Independence for their return. Even if the Chávezes did not purchase goods in town their eastward travels were fine with the farmers and various craftsmen. For they got to refit the wagons and feed the horses and oxen, and most importantly the townsfolk would be paid in silver when the Chávezes returned.

Early in the undistinguished year of 1843, the Chávezes were preparing another trading excursion to Missouri. In the fall of 1842 rumors began to circulate in New Mexico about a newly formed band of lawless men. Furthermore these distant rumblings mentioned that these outlaws were masquerading as Texans and were intent on raiding Mexican merchants in the coming spring. In January the governor of New Mexico learned from the U.S. Consul in Santa Fe that one Col. Warfield, of the Texas army, had taken command of this band and was preparing a foray to sweep the Santa Fe Trail clear of Mexican merchants and then invade Mexico.

Paying special attention to the rumors of raiders along their route, the Chávezes decided to risk an early March trip led by Antonio José to Independence. Such a venture also ran the danger of either random attacks by Indians or being surprised by a spring blizzard while on the open trail. These major snowstorms could decimate a caravan caught in their frigid fierce winds. It happened, in November 1841, to a small party commanded by the U.S. Consul heading toward Independence. In this tragic mishap two men died and all the pack animals perished.

Business was booming and the brothers expected a very profitable year. The risk seemed worth the financial rewards to the Chávez family. Antonio José was to start out early, shoot past Independence and make for St. Louis and points further east. Once he had purchased all the manufactured goods that his money could buy, he was to transport the wares by rail and steamboat to Independence. All this was to be accomplished in time to rendezvous with the American caravan leaving for Santa Fe in May. The strategy was evolved to avoid any confrontation with the rumored "Texas raiders."

Whether McDaniel actually knew that Antonio José planned to arrive early in Independence or he found the Mexican company by accident is the subject of considerable debate. Most of the contemporary sources believe that what happened on the deserted plains of Kansas was a cold, premeditated act. To this end Col. Henry Inman, an experienced plainsman wrote in his book, *The Old Santa Fe Trail*, that John McDaniel sent spies out on the trail to warn him of Antonio José's coming.

It was not exactly a secret that something was about to happen. Several of the men recruited by Warfield, but repulsed by McDaniel's personality, left the gang and began spreading rumors of a planned raid on an unnamed Mexican merchant. After a while everyone in Independence suspected that one of Chávezes would be the intended victim. On April Fools' Day the McDaniel gang left Yoacham's Tavern and unknowingly rode into history, albeit if only to become a footnote.

On or about March 15, Antonio José rode into the Unorganized Territories with 20 men, a dozen mules and two wagons. Somewhere in what is now Kansas, between the Cimarron and Arkansas rivers, his small caravan ran into a cold front accompanied by a severe snowstorm. Fifteen men came down with bad cases of frostbite. Most of his mules died. A majority of the stricken men deserted Chávez and hobbled back to Santa Fe. This left Antonio José with five men and enough mules to pull one wagon. But he was not deterred by this unfortunate occurrence and traveled onward toward Independence and his ultimate misfortune.

On April 1 Chávez sent one his servants ahead by

For the Missouri boarder towns the Santa Fe Trail meant economic survival. In 1843 a Mexican was found murdered on the trail and disaster loomed on the horizon.

mule to get help. With lightning speed McDaniel and his gang, not knowing of Antonio José's misfortune, rode toward the beleaguered party. The raiders averaged 30 miles a day, the servant, riding a mule, made less time. Both the servant and McDaniel's gang were bound to meet each other on the trail. The rendezvous occurred somewhere in eastern Kansas. At first the servant thought these men were coming to aid his master. He told them approximately where Antonio José was, and the quandary his master was in. John McDaniel immediately took him prisoner. The servant was forced to lead the gang to the approximate place where Chávez and his men were struggling toward Missouri.

On either April 8 or 9 McDaniel's gang encountered Antonio José's troubled caravan at Owl Creek. As viewed from the air, Owl Creek was a small 10 mile long bush-covered gully. It was a tiny undistinguished crease in the earth that ran north/south, crossing the Santa Fe Trail about 250 miles west of Independence.

The caravan was taken completely by surprise. Before they could protest, McDaniel's gang hustled the Mexicans and the wagon off the trail to a secluded area several miles south on Owl Creek.

Quickly the bandits ransacked the wagon. Arguments broke out over how to share the silver coins, gold and small furs. A whole day was spent arguing and dividing the loot. In the end each gang member received $500 per share. No mention was made whether or not the McDaniel brothers received more than one share, but likely they did. Never was there mention of saving half the spoils for the Republic of Texas. So much for Warfield's patriotic dream of adventure; it had become a pedestrian crime.

At this juncture John McDaniel had a brainstorm that would split his bandit band in half. He reasoned if Antonio José were to be set free, the Mexican would keep traveling east toward Independence and not run home in shame. Once Chávez reached the town he would report the robbery to the proper authorities. Once the crime was known McDaniel and his gang would be declared outlaws. So the best way to protect his gang was to kill the Mexican merchant.

Dr. Joseph R. De Prefontaine headed the opposition. He was indeed a medical doctor as his title suggests. But his expensive tastes led him into a dual life. In public he was one of the prominent men in St. Louis society; in private he was a scheming con man. He had a taste for the good life and he didn't

Despite its sleepy town appearance, Santa Fe was Northern Mexico's commercial center. Silver pesos and gold doubloons flowed from Santa Fe along the Santa Fe Trail and stabilized the rural Missouri economy.

realize that the life he was leading was already quite good. The known Dr. Prefontaine was a man who would work at the request of the Indian Department for a peanut sized wage inoculating various tribes against smallpox. The unknown doctor would present false medical bills at the settlement of estates that came before the court. Eventually this swindle and his other scams ran out of steam. In 1842 he found his house and belongings sold out from under him to satisfy his creditors. Leaving St. Louis in disgrace, he migrated to the frontier. It has been assumed that Dr. Prefontaine met John McDaniel at Yoachim's Tavern later that year. The promise of easy riches must have been too much of a temptation for the fallen doctor, so he joined the gang.

Now came the time for Dr. Prefontaine to take a stand. He was a doctor; he was bound by oath to save lives, not to take them. Dr. Prefontaine said that stealing the gold, silver and furs were bad enough, he would not add murder to his list of crimes. John McDaniel loudly repeated his reasons for killing Antonio José; if Dr. Prefontaine was so worried about this crime then killing the merchant was the best way to keep the crime and identities secret. Dr. Prefontaine probably would have been shot by McDaniel had he objected alone, but half the gang agreed with him. An argument broke out.

It turned out to be an acrimonious debate. When night fell McDaniel told the protesting faction to leave in the morning. This was fine with Dr. Prefontaine and his followers, but there turned out to be one unexpected hitch. That night while the gang slept, the horses and mules stampeded. No one ever claimed the animals had an opinion on the subject of Antonio José's planned murder, they just acted as if they did and fled.

A few hours after sunrise the gang split up. Dr. Prefontaine and those that sided with him walked back to Independence carrying their heavy plunder on their backs. Those who remained at the Owl Creek camp discussed who would do the dastardly deed. Not everyone shared their leader's enthusiasm for murder. Thomas Towson and the Searcy brothers, Nathaniel and Christopher, objected to being one of the executioners. McDaniel settled the matter by deciding they would all draw straws to see who would kill the Mexican. There were to be no exceptions. No one dared find out what the penalty was for refusing.

The "winners" of the grotesque lottery were the McDaniel brothers, one of the Searcy brothers and William Mason. In the interests of keeping peace, Joseph Brown offered to stand in for the Searcy brother who drew the unlucky short straw.

The merchant's servants were taken behind a hill, out of sight of the events to follow. John McDaniel took Chávez for a walk, closely followed by the other members of the execution squad. The two men walked 150 feet away from the camp. Antonio José's attention was held by the casual conversation he was having with his captor. Suddenly McDaniel pulled a gun and shot the Mexican at point blank range in the chest. According to one account, the wounded Antonio José dodged bullets as he sprinted for 300 feet before being tripped by the pursuing McDaniel and finally killed by the gang. The more plausible version, considering that Chávez had a bullet in his chest, was that he ran about a yard or two before being cut down by a volley of bullets. Later, at the trial, there was a question of who fired the fatal shot or shots. William Mason, who would later turn states evidence at the trial, presented his account with some significant differences.

As Mason recalled the events, and as collaborated by Towson, Antonio José ran a few yards, was tripped by John McDaniel and shot as he lay on the ground. The rest of the gang gathered around the prostrate Mexican and pumped the body full of bullets. Mason claimed to have fired the last shot after the Mexican was already dead; it was a shot fired in fear. Mason felt if he didn't fire his pistol at the dead man, he might have been the next to be killed.

Before the killers moved Antonio José's body, it was searched. A hidden money belt was found containing almost 40 gold coins. Fortune seemed to be smiling on the slayers so they decided to reexamine the merchant's wagon. Inside a trunk they discovered a secret compartment which concealed a little over $3,000 in gold dust.

McDaniel was now in a good mood. In a pretense of generosity, he let the retainers go. He did this for several reasons. In the first place he thought the docile servants would meekly return to Santa Fe. In the second place he was sure that if roving bands of Indians didn't kill the unarmed Mexicans the unpredictable and severe weather would. Just to be on the safe side McDaniel did not bother to leave the servants with any food or water.

After the Mexicans were chased from the Owl Creek camp the gang unceremoniously dumped Antonio José's body in a nearby ravine. McDaniel's thieving outfit walked up Owl Creek to the point where it meets the Santa Fe Trail. Much to their amazement they found nine of the stampeded horses freely grazing by the side of the trail. And so the gang mounted up and used the spare horse to carry much of the plunder. It would seem that nothing could possibly wrong that day.

At first McDaniel rode toward Point of Rocks, the location of his planned rendezvous with Warfield. But after few days of easy riding McDaniel claimed to have seen signs of Indians on the trail. Not wanting to tempt fate any further the gang abruptly turned around and rode back toward Independence. While the McDaniel gang was out on the lonesome plains, related events were taking shape and gathering momentum.

The rumors that circulated on the frontier before the thieves left Yoachim's Tavern began to have an effect. Superintendent Mitchell of Indian Affairs in St. Louis was notified of the gang's intentions on March 13. His office presided over the various tribes and exercised civil authority over United States citizens in the Indian Territory. To enforce the law, Mitchell had at his command the U.S. Army. Unfortunately he was a pure bureaucrat and would not move any faster than absolutely necessary. To his credit, the superintendent did interview Warfield sometime in early April. In a letter, dated April 21, to the United States Secretary of War, he wrote that the colonel had no intention of committing crimes against Americans on the Santa Fe Trail, but he felt that any Mexicans not within United States borders were fair game. To his discredit, Mitchell ended the letter by saying it was not for him to give any opinion on the Warfield matter, he was just passing the information along to proper areas of government.

While Mitchell, the man in charge of all Indian Territories, was doing almost nothing, his subordinate, Indian Agent R.W. Cummins, stationed near Independence, took action. Cummins heard about McDaniel's plans from the town's residents and merchants. He quickly sent a message to Col. Richard B. Mason at Fort Leavenworth, 30 miles away. The colonel responded with equal speed. Three days later he sent a detachment of 60 cavalrymen to find McDaniel and his gang.

The soldiers searched the Santa Fe Trail as far as their week's worth of rations would take them. Afterwards some citizens would claim that the army ended their search for the outlaws one day's ride short of finding McDaniel. Such critical hindsight ignores the most practical aspect of an army—they really do travel on their stomachs. A soldier's effectiveness drops as his supplies diminish. Without food for a longer foray into the Indian Territories, the cavalry traveled as far as they could.

Although the cavalry did not find evidence of any wrongdoing, people in Missouri suspected that trouble was brewing. Col. Stephen Watts Kearny, commander of the Third Military Department, was taking no chances. He sent three more companies of cavalry, two more from Fort Leavenworth and one from Fort Scott. Their orders were to escort any caravan through the Indian Territories, regardless of their nationality.

Kearny wanted to go a step further; he wanted to accompany the caravans across the Mexican border as far as Santa Fe. Militarily this made sense; politically it was naive. The U.S. secretary of war and the Mexican ambassador conferred on the matter. Although the ambassador was in favor of U.S. Army escorts to the border, he was unwilling to have foreign troops marching into Mexico. As a result of the conference Kearny was ordered not to cross the Mexican boundary. It didn't really matter. The McDaniel gang had already struck, and soon all of Missouri would know about it.

Rueben and Nicholas Gentry were cousins and traders. Each had their own business and each had a stake in maintaining the status quo along the Santa Fe Trail. In mid-March, Rueben had just delivered 12 wagon loads of English goods to Santa Fe when he learned of Antonio José's early departure. Unwilling to wait for the April 1 caravan bound for Independence, Rueben left Santa Fe with only a one day stopover to replenish his supplies.

His small party made good time on the trail. Somewhere in the first third of their trek through the endless Kansas prairie, Gentry came across several of Chávez's frostbitten servants. He learned of the Mexican's dire circumstances after the snowstorm, but not about his abduction. This news drove Rueben harder. In central Kansas, beyond the Great Bend, the party found Antonio José's last trail-side campfire. Rueben thought they were about a day's ride behind Chávez. But the next day he arrived at Owl Creek and found that the Mexican's wagon tracks went off the trail toward the south. At the time Rueben thought Antonio José took a shortcut that he was not familiar with. So the small company rode even faster on the trail to catch up with Chávez. The next day Rueben became worried. There were no more signs of the Mexican party on the trail. At the very least Gentry should have seen the resumption of fresh wagon tracks.

Gentry correctly made two following assumptions: first, Chávez had met with foul play; second, whoever was responsible for the treachery outnumbered his small party. Being ambushed on the trail was not Rueben's idea of having fun, so he quit looking for signs of Chávez and quickly rode to Independence with his terrible news. Later Gentry was to learn that while he was contemplating Antonio José's abrupt departure from the trail at Owl Creek, Chávez was several miles down the gully being robbed. He was also correct in assuming that there was nothing he could have done against McDaniel's 14 well armed men.

While Gentry was making his way toward Missouri, Dr. Prefontaine's group had reached the Santa Fe Trail and was following behind on foot. Neither group was aware of the other's presence. The thieves made it as far Council Grove before the weight of their booty became too much to carry. Dr. Prefontaine decided that they should bury the loot nearby and retrieve it later when it was safe. The plunder hidden the band split into smaller groups, each making its separate ways toward Missouri.

On April 19 Rueben arrived at Independence and spread the word of Antonio José's disappearance. The next day all the Missouri newspapers carried the story. Independence and nearby Westport residents reacted immediately by forming posses to search for Chávez. One such group was headed by William Gilpin. Gilpin was a well educated Quaker who had been tutored as a child by Nathaniel Hawthorne. In 1861 he would become the first governor of the Colorado Territory.

It was Gilpin's company that found Antonio José's wagon on Owl Creek 5 miles south of the Santa Fe Trail. No corpse was found and it was presumed that wolves had discovered Chávez before the posse found the wagon. Years later Gilpin would say that his party did find patches of human hair, but had no idea at the time that it belonged to Antonio José.

John McDaniel did not have to bury his spoils as Dr. Prefontaine did. His group carried the loot to Independence on their horses. To make themselves as inconspicuous as possible the gang split up into smaller groups at the frontier. The most successful of these parties was the Searcy brothers. According to the newspapers, they took a steamer upriver from Westport Landing to Park's Landing, debarked and disappeared into the heartland forever.

The McDaniel brothers were less fortunate. They were recognized by Rueben Gentry. On his way to make his report at Fort Leavenworth, Gentry had taken the same steamer as the Searcy brothers. He failed to recognize them the first time, but on his return trip to Independence Rueben noticed three suspicious looking men board the paddlewheeler at the last moment. Why these men stood out in Gentry's mind will never be known. Maybe it was their distrustful manner, perhaps it was the way they bounded out of the shadows and boarded the boat, or maybe it was the two bundles of fur they carried with them. The skins were beaver, exactly the kind that the Mexicans usually traded.

Reuben soon discovered that his suspicions were correct. After watching the three men for several minutes, Gentry walked over to the clerk's office and scanned the boat's passenger list. Reuben knew who he was looking for, because when he was making his report at Fort Leavenworth Reuben was told about Warfield's recruitment activities and McDaniel's

FIERCE BANDITS AT BAY.

In the East the frontier was portrayed as dangerous, uncivilized land, full of unsavory characters who would steal your money as soon as look at you. In fact compared to the respectable cities like New York, the frontier was usually downright boring.

planned robbery of Antonio José. If there was foul play, McDaniel and his gang were prime suspects. As his gaze fell upon the ledger three signatures stood out, "John McDaniel for Texas, David McDaniel and William Mason."

McDaniel had signed his real name when he boarded the steamboat because he had no idea he was wanted for his crimes. He was just being his obnoxious self. He soon found out how dire his circumstance really was.

Two developments occurred simultaneously when the paddlewheeler stopped at Independence Landing. Gentry sent an urgent note to Independence, two miles away, stating that the McDaniels and Mason were aboard the steamboat. Included in the note was a plan for the authorities to meet the

boat down river at Owens Landing. This stop was 15 miles away by water, owing to a large bend in the river, but only six miles by horse, owing to a straight land route. At the same time John McDaniel heard from some of the passengers that his crime was common knowledge and he was a wanted man.

The McDaniel brothers quickly devised a plan of their own. When the steamboat briefly landed at their hometown of Liberty, the brothers debarked. Due to heavy rains, the spring floods had swollen the Missouri and knocked out all ferry service across the river for several weeks. The only boat capable of navigating the river was the paddlewheeler. From the frontier to St. Louis, Liberty was the only stop on the north side of the Missouri River. By all rights they should have at least a week's lead on any posse

The citizens of St. Louis were only too happy to host the trial of the McDaniel gang. After all these men almost severed their economic jugular vein.

pursuing them.

Gentry's plan was only partially successful. The good news was that as soon as the townsfolk heard about McDaniel brothers' whereabouts, a 20-man posse formed and rode to Owens Landing. They arrived just as the paddlewheeler was about to shove off. The vigilantes clamored aboard as soon as the boat was stopped. Reuben Gentry met them and together they searched the ship for the wanted men. Mason was their only catch. He still had Chávez's beaver furs with him. According to some of the passengers Mason had tossed something overboard just before the posse found him. A few men from the posse dove into the fast moving river and after a few minutes of searching brought up nine Mexican gold coins, which were laying on top of the mud.

Mason was shown the evidence and interrogated. In a matter of minutes he confessed to the robbery. A few moments later he told Gentry that Antonio José was murdered. What began as a dribble became a torrent and Mason just babbled on and on. He described the murder to the minutest detail, including

how he fired the last shot after Chávez was dead.

Mason was escorted back to the Independence jail by two members of the posse. All the way along the six-mile route the bandit kept rambling on about his small part in the crime and about his fear and loathing of McDaniel. He would later testify against his former gang leader.

The flooded river prevented news of Chávez's murder from getting to the isolated town and the McDaniel brothers felt safe in their hometown. As luck would have it, one of Prefontaine's men, Samuel Berry, had arrived in Liberty a few days earlier. He told the townsfolk who knew of McDaniel's plans that signs of an Indian war party in Kansas forced the company back. Berry added, the expedition was a failure and they never joined up with Warfield. Later, when McDaniel heard the story, he chuckled and concurred with Berry's version and went about his business.

What McDaniel did not realize was that the posse was still very determined to catch him. They persuaded the captain of the paddlewheeler to briefly change his itinerary and land on the northern shore of the river. He agreed to take only 10 men with their horses. Three days later the unexpected posse rode into town and with them came the surprising truth of McDaniel's activities. Even the citizens of Liberty had a stake in the Missouri/Mexican trade arrangement, and they were quick to tell the posse where the McDaniel brothers could be found.

McDaniel was caught while crossing Liberty's main street. A small number of the posse, perhaps two or three, rode toward McDaniel calling out his name. As he turned toward the riders, he started to reach for his pistol. At that very moment the rest of the posse appeared with guns already drawn. McDaniel saw he didn't have a chance, so he put his hands up and was captured. His brother and Berry were also arrested the same day. All three of them were taken to the Independence jail, where the talkative Mason was residing.

Maybe it was his proximity to Mason, but once Berry was in custody he began talk. Closely matching his fellow gang member and jail mate's version, Berry told his interrogators where the Prefontaine splinter group buried their share of the loot near Council Grove.

Rueben Gentry's cousin, Nicholas, took charge of the posse that went after the plunder. "Old Nick," as many knew him, was quite a character. His wry sense of humor always served him well whether he was trading for himself or working for others. In Mexico he had another pseudonym. They knew him as "Old Contraband Gentry" for his incredible ability to smuggle goods past the customs officials. Nicholas had searched for McDaniel too, but his group looked for the gang leader in the country near Independence. Now it was his chance to gain some of the fame his cousin had gathered.

About 100 miles from Independence, Nicholas' posse met two men riding toward Missouri. One of them was none other than Dr. Prefontaine himself, and his companion was the tavern owner, Daniel Yoacham. Quickly the errant doctor was taken into custody. In his possession the posse found all of the buried booty. It seems Dr. Prefontaine had no qualms when it came to stealing from his fellow thieves. Yoacham was also arrested, but later released in Independence for lack of criminal intent. However, Yoacham lived under a cloud of suspicion that would hover over him for the rest of his days. Many believed there was no way that Yoacham did not know what McDaniel and his gang was up to, and some even believed that he was part of the gang.

Less than a week after the search started, 10 members of McDaniel's gang were behind bars. Five men escaped including the Searcy brothers. A little

over $7,000 in furs, gold and silver was recovered. From the approximate amount outstanding, the sheriff in Independence estimated that Antonio José was carrying about $11,000 in valuables at the time of his abduction.

Since the crime occurred in the Unorganized or Indian Territories, jurisdiction in this matter fell to the U.S. Circuit Court in the District of Missouri, which was located in St. Louis. Everyone was anxious to start the trial as soon as possible. Preliminary hearings were held on May 3, even before the McDaniel brothers were brought to the St. Louis jail. Three weeks later all 10 of the captured men were together in the same jail. To the puzzlement of the prosecutors and defense attorneys alike, the prisoners exhibited an unexpected confidence that they would be released as soon as the truth were known.

Newspapers countrywide became embroiled in the controversy. The McDaniel gang justified Chávez's murder by claiming that they had committed an act of legal reprisal against Mexico. By their reasoning, John McDaniel's commission as a captain in the Texas army was all the excuse they needed for the foul play visited upon the Mexican merchant.

The murder of Antonio José provoked a stormy national debate. A chorus of broadsides, pro and con, were published throughout the land. "McDaniel and his party are innocent. They had a commission and it was only a Mexican they killed. Chávez was on American territory therefore protected by the law. It was an act of undeclared war between Texas and Mexico and therefore legal from the Texan point of view. Commission or no, a crime was committed and the gang must pay the price."

The most outrageous statement came from a New York City newspaper. Its editorial claimed that it should come as no surprise that such a crime was committed, since as everyone knows, there were many Missourians who made a living robbing Santa Fe Mexicans and Indians.

The eastern portion of the country believed the frontier was a wild and lawless place. No one ever went to jail in that god-forsaken land, no matter how villainous the crime. People in New York believed this with an air of moral superiority. They held this notion even though the worst American urban sewer of depravity was found in Manhattan and it was called The Five Points.

Just when it seemed as if McDaniel's trial would involve some cut-and-dry issues, a new chorus of disclaimers arose from the Republic of Texas. In essence they said Warfield had no part in Chávez's killing since McDaniel and his gang never joined the colonel's raiding party. Some uninformed newspapers even denied Warfield ever gave McDaniel a commission at all.

The political issues became murkier when it was reported that 17 men were executed by the Mexican army. These Texans were members of the party who invaded Mexico in pursuit of the army that took part in the short capture of San Antonio.

During the summer months, while the gang cooled their heels in jail, the wheels of justice slowly began to turn. Bail was denied to all of the arrested men. The prosecutor in the case maneuvered to have everyone tried for murder. He lost. On September 16 the indictments were handed down and those who left with Dr. Prefontaine were only charged with larceny. Both groups were charged with illegally organizing a military expedition on American soil. McDaniel and party were indicted for murder.

Dr. Prefontaine and those who left with him were tried almost immediately in Jefferson City. He was found guilty, and perhaps because he was a likable fellow, he was sentenced to a year in jail and a $1,000 fine. In the matter of the other men, the jury was hung. It was decided to retry them the following April in St. Louis. April was the same month that the McDaniel gang trial was scheduled to start.

United States Attorney William M. McPherson had one objective: to make McDaniel and his gang pay for their crimes. McPherson was not about to lose his prime witnesses, so his first action was to have Chávez's servants comfortably held in the St. Louis jail from September until April. To make their stay more agreeable, the Mexicans were paid over $350 for their time, and five cents per mile for their return to Santa Fe.

In April McPherson dispatched Dr. Prefontaine's gang with a round of plea bargaining. In return for the guilty pleas, the thieves were each sentenced to nine months in jail and a $10 fine. Berry was freed after he testified against the McDaniel gang. Nothing was going to interfere with the murder trial, all the extraneous business was going to be cleared up. Nothing was going to cloud the issues. McPherson was going to get his conviction.

A parade of prosecution witnesses testified before the jury. They included the Gentrys, various merchants, traders, Dr. Prefontaine, Samuel O. Berry and Chávez's servants. The Mexicans' testimony, given in Spanish and translated for the court into English, substantiated the eyewitness testimonies of Thomas Towson and William Mason. Now it was the defense's turn.

Edward Bates, McDaniel's lawyer, attempted to use the Warfield Texas army commission as a mitigating circumstance, but the judge wouldn't allow that argument. He had two justifications for refusing that line of defense: the commission could not be produced by McDaniel and acts of military reprisal do not include homicide on U.S. soil.

With one potent legal weapon gone, the defense turned to discrediting McPherson's main witness, William Mason. Bates correctly speculated that if he went after the mentally defective Towson the jury would immediately turn on his client.

Mason was successfully portrayed as unreliable by the defense. The jury almost believed that it was Mason who abandoned the McDaniel brothers aboard the paddlewheeler and not the other way around. Bates even attempted to show that it was Mason who killed Antonio José. But this success was mitigated by the other testimony given by Towson and Chávez's servants because it corroborated with Mason's testimony on all the crucial points. No matter how bad Mason's character was, the jury believed his story and the guilty verdict brought in against the four defendants.

The McDaniel brothers and Joseph Brown were sentenced to hang on June 14. Thomas Towson received a suspended sentence, as the court declared him mentally defective and incapable of making important decisions for himself. Because he turned state's evidence, Mason was not prosecuted in return for his testimony.

The energetic Bates tried every possible means to overturn the convictions. His strongest argument was that United States government did not have jurisdiction beyond the Missouri boarder. The appeal was denied. Next he petitioned President Tyler for clemency. This resulted in a series of presidential stays of execution. John McDaniel and Brown had their hanging postponed until July 12, and then until August 16. David McDaniel's execution was put off until June 27, 1845.

As all condemned men do, McDaniel and Brown believed up until the last moment that they would get another reprieve. But when the August 16 arrived and no further word was received from Washington, they knew their time had run out. Usually a hanging was a family affair with picnics and other entertainments. But it seems that many of the townspeople also thought the murderers would get another stay of execution, so only several thousand showed up for the hanging.

At 2 o'clock McDaniel and Brown were led up the scaffold and read their death sentences. Each man gave a final speech proclaiming his innocence, and then the pair were hanged together. They paid the ultimate price for their greedy folly.

David McDaniel was luckier. Since his execution was delayed for so long, President Tyler had time to reflect upon McDaniel's age and the probability that his older, recently executed brother had unduly in-

In an age where families could not sit at home in front of the television and watch the latest in Texas Chainsaw whatever, hangings
were the next best form of entertainment. Everyone in town usually
showed, some with picnic baskets, some selling wares. For McDaniel
and Brown's hanging only few thousand appeared. Popular wisdom
at the time believed they would receive yet another reprieve.

When roused to action, the citizens of this prosperous little frontier town moved swiftly to apprehend the McDaniel Gang.

fluenced the young man. He decided to pardon David. The surviving McDaniel brother left Missouri and was never heard from again.

After serving his prison sentence, Dr. Prefontaine drifted further west. Sometime during the heyday of the California gold rush he was discovered in the lobby of the El Dorado hotel by Capt. James Hobbs. Hobbs was employed at the time as a scout and helped Nicholas Gentry track down the errant doctor. To the former scout's amazement, Prefontaine had become a prominent citizen and the editor of a San Francisco scandal sheet. Hobbs kept Dr. Prefontaine's crime a secret until the doctor's death in the late 1860s.

Warfield's expedition met with disaster. The colonel never received his expected reinforcements from Texas and Missouri. Not one to be deterred, he began his invasion of New Mexico with a small company who had gathered at Point of Rocks. In an amazingly ineffectual attack, Warfield managed to disperse a small Mexican troop, killing five of the soldiers in the process. A few days after the Mexicans counterattacked, driving off all of the raider's horses, he retreated eastward. Warfield's dreams of glory ended in ignominy, and he retreated on foot 200 miles to the north. Several weeks later he arrived at Bent's Fort where he disbanded his men.

For several years the Santa Fe Trail trade suffered. The first year was the worst. Warfield's failure prompted another adventurer, Col. Jacob Snively, to attempt the same plan. This began a series of small engagements on Mexican territory and the Santa Fe Trail. Snively's "Invincibles" won a major skirmish against the Mexican army. Commerce on the Santa Fe Trail had come to a halt. Finally the U.S. Army was sent out and disarmed Snively's bunch. The economies of both Santa Fe and Missouri fell into dismal disarray.

Eventually trade on the Santa Fe Trail returned to normal a year later and wagons eagerly plied the road once more. After that, the Mexican War trade continued, although at a diminished rate. New Mexico could no longer offer Mexican silver and gold because it was now United States territory. Missouri would enjoy another economic boom with the coming of the "Forty Niners." Tens of thousands of the gold rushers wintered along the frontier waiting to make their mad dash toward California in the spring. Missouri was only to happy to take the Argonaut's money for supplies and shelter.

One last word must be said regarding Owl Creek. The honest folk of Missouri changed the gully's name in honor of the slain merchant. Unfortunately they did not speak Spanish and the name Chávez became distorted over time: Chavis, Chauvey, Charvis, Garvis and finally Jarvis. Jarvis is the name it is known by today.

1891

Even in the Best of Families and the Best of Places

George Abbott was born in 1857 in New England. The town where he spent his childhood considered "Abbott" to be a "long sustained and honored name." Three days after his birth, his mother died. This was not an unusual occurrence in those days; a cursory glance at the headstones of the era bear cold witness to this fact. His father was too successful and busy with business to raise a child, so George was adopted by his aunt and uncle, Mr. and Mrs. Israel Abbott of Salem, Massachusetts.

His formal education began at the Brown School, a boarding institution. When George was 10 his adopted parents moved to their farm in North Thetford, Vermont, and young Abbott found himself going to a public school. It was here at the age of 11 that he began his life of crime.

At first young Abbott found items such as jack-knives, pens and pencils just fell into his pockets and stayed there. He was a juvenile thief. But he wasn't some dumb student trying to kill time until he could leave school; George was a good student. Early in his schooling he had learned to read faster then most of his contemporaries. Unfortunately, his tastes in literature ran more in the vein of dime novels than the classics. He was popular with his classmates, and perhaps only a handful suspected him of having larcenous tendencies.

As a boy grows his habits change, and soon Abbott escalated his thefts to include jewelry and watches. Most of his booty was carefully hidden in a cave he had dug in the Vermont bank of the Connecticut River. It was a shrine and museum of Abbott's ill-gotten gains. His career came to an abrupt suspension at the age of 14, when he was caught with a stolen cast-iron stove in his possession.

His absent father came to North Thetford and succeeded in manipulating the justice system, the way that wealthy and influential men can do. All the charges against his son were dropped. However, young Abbott was not content with being kept out of reform school. He wanted revenge and he got it. George shot his accuser's dog in the head and killed it. To forestall any unwanted consequences for this act he threatened the owner. Things got a bit messy for a while, but then the victim decided to cool off and let the matter drop. More than likely he was afraid of George.

Around this time young Abbott dropped out of school and worked on the family farm. It was here that he met a farmhand named Pete Duplissy. They started to hang around together and chew tobacco. If Abbott came from a noble family, Duplissy's kin were known as petty criminals, or in the words of the upright citizens of North Thetford, the Duplissy family was a "mess of egg-sucking, doughnut-robbing, cigaroot-smoking scallawags."

By the time he was 17, Abbott and Duplissy were burglarizing the better homes in the area. They were eventually caught with gold pins, cash, silver watches, gallons of booze and burglar tools in their possession. On November 5, 1874, Abbott was sentenced to four years at the New Hampshire penitentiary in Concord.

In the best of families young Abbott's crimes would have constituted a great disgrace. And Abbott's father came from the best of families. Rather than face his friends and associates as the father of a criminal, and rather than hear imaginary whispers of shame for the rest of his days, he hanged himself. In his will he left his wealth to his son, hoping it would change George's ways when he got out of prison, hoping his son would spend the money to erase the dishonor he had brought upon the family name.

In 1878 Abbott emerged from prison an older

George Abbott was born into an old and venerated New England families. These are those few families who can trace their lineage in America to landing of the Mayflower. But families change a lot in four hundred years and every so often a "bad seed" grows from good stock. New Englanders considered George Abbott to be such a misfit.

and wiser criminal. Quickly he proceeded to claim his inheritance, about $5,000, and run through it in less than a year, on booze, women and anything else that struck his fancy. In the summer of 1879 a broke and, to all appearances, humble George Abbott showed up at Uncle Israel's farm and went back to working as a farmhand. The haying season over he walked into the hills and disappeared.

About the time of Abbott's disappearance an odd series of professional burglaries began occurring in the Greater North Thetford area. No establishment was safe. Stores, homes, barns, schools, all but the post office were robbed of their valuables. The police from all the area towns began to search for the thief or thieves. Everyone believed young Abbott was responsible, but no one had seen him for over a year.

Fate moves in strange and mysterious ways. Mark Ware grew up on his family farm. He was not old enough to vote in an age when most Americans felt it was their sacred duty to do so. On Election Day, November 1880, the day that James A. Garfield and Chester A. Arthur were being elected to the office of president and vice president, respectively, Mark decided to explore Thetford mountain. He made an important discovery.

Mark had climbed for a good part of the morning when he accidently discovered a little used trail hidden by some overgrown bushes. He followed the trail until it emerged upon a clearing on the river side of the mountain. Standing on the cliff, Mark could see the vast panorama of the Connecticut River Valley below. Ware noticed that had he not found the trail this place would have been inaccessible from any other direction. Yet much to his surprise he found cigarette butts and other evidence of human habitation. Further investigation of the area revealed a hand-dug cave. Ware carefully explored the cave and discovered a treasure-trove of plunder. There was jewelry, watches, silverware, furniture and a few burglar tools hanging on a wall, which clearly indicated that these were ill-gotten gains.

The teenager was fascinated by one tool in particular, a bull's-eye lantern. This was a small coal oil burning affair with a sliding shutter and a thick glass lens to focus the light into a narrow beam, much like one gets from a modern flashlight. Later, when law enforcement officers had a chance to catalog the loot, it was discovered that Abbott had kept much of the plunder he had stolen since he was 11 years old.

Young Ware made several mental notes as to the

location of the cave and then ran to town to report his discovery. The sheriff rounded up a large posse armed with shotguns and rifles. But it was already dark by the time everyone was notified so they put off their search until morning.

Morning dawned clear, crisp and bright, the kind of Vermont weather that many of the posse would look forward to during deer hunting season. Today's quarry ran on two legs and had already outsmarted them for over a year. If Abbott was spotted, the posse agreed upon firing their rifles into the air as a signal. The other searchers would rush to the area and hopefully the young thief would be caught.

Sometime in the early afternoon Abbott's luck ran out. He came across two men with rifles walking through the Thetford mountain woods. The men were surprised to see him and seemed a little nervous, perhaps because he also was carrying a rifle. When he asked them what they were doing in the woods they replied, "squirrel hunting." One thing led to another, and from the men's bantering a contest developed to see who was the best shot. It was decided the winner would be whoever hit a particular small knot on a tree.

Abbott fired first and hit the mark, the two hunters fired next and missed. The sound of the shots echoed through the mountain and before another contest could be devised Abbott found himself surrounded by a dozen armed men.

Abbott was no fool; he quickly surmised what had really happened. He may have berated himself for being tricked into idiotically firing his rifle on the quiet mountain side and attracting attention, but the matter at hand was his escape. A thin grin grew on his face as he fired at the nearest posse member and broke into a low sprint across the mountain. Abbott's shot missed its target, but several of the hunters were excellent shots. Three shots brought him down, one in the leg and two in the chest. Abbott fell to the ground, badly wounded and many thought close to death.

That night, a sickly pale Abbott lay in a room requisitioned by the North Thetford sheriff. The sheriff sat by the dying man until he was called away for a some small matter. Abbott was left unattended for less than five minutes, but in that time he managed to get out of bed and climb out the window. Another posse was organized and by mid-afternoon he was found under a railroad culvert, naked except for a quilt, half frozen yet still alive.

In the spring of 1881 Abbott was sentenced to 15 years incarceration, to be served at Windsor Prison, Vermont. Windsor Prison was a stone-hard anachronism of its time. The idea of imprisonment as a form of punishment was a fairly recent devel-

opment in modern history. Until the late 18th century prisons were used to confine debtors and accused persons awaiting trial, and convicted persons awaiting death or exile. Lesser crimes requiring less than one year's confinement were the only sentences which were carried out in a prison.

In the early United States fines and imprisonment became the major form of punishment for all criminal offenses. In 1794 the converted Walnut Street Jail in Philadelphia became the first state penitentiary in the new nation. Hard labor was the rule, and it was applied harshly.

In the early 19th century a new wrinkle was added to the concept of imprisonment, the silent system. Under this system prisoners were allowed to work together during the daytime, but they could not talk to each other while they toiled. At night the prisoners were bedded in solitary cells with no one to converse with. By the 1880s many new penology reforms were making inroads in the American prison system, but the winds of change had blown into Windsor, Vermont. This was the kind of prison that not-so-young George Abbott was sentenced to.

Any man who kept his earliest plunder as trophies in a cleverly camouflaged, hand-hewn cave can safely be called patient and resourceful. As soon as he arrived at Windsor Prison Abbott began to plot his escape. This was to be no minor feat since the prison was known to be escape-proof. Abbott's plan was simple: first, he found all the discarded thread, string and cord available; second, he wove these disparate pieces into two long ropes; third, taking advantage of his jobs in the engine and boiler rooms, he stole short lengths of metal tubing; forth, he inserted the tubing into the lengths of rope, turning it into a sturdy ladder. It took six patient years to complete this ladder, and six years in prison was all Abbott wanted to stay.

On the night of September 30, 1887, at 7:45 p.m. George Abbott rang the engine room bell. It was a signal which told the warden and the prison guards that he was at his post. At 8:00 p.m. there was no bell. When the guards investigated the cause for this omission they found that George Abbott had scaled the prison wall and climbed down the other side on his handmade ladder.

Thirty-year-old George Abbott did more than escape from prison, he ceased to exist. In his place appeared Frank Almy. Where Abbott had served a third of his life in prison, Almy claimed to have spent most of his life wandering the country working at odd jobs.

During the next few years Almy/Abbott worked his way up and down the East Coast doing odd jobs. Sometime in 1889 he appeared in Massachusetts;

Almy/Abbott was back in New England to stay. On July 11, 1890 Frank Almy wandered into Hanover and took a job as a hired hand on the farm of Andrew Warden. Hanover is a town located along the Connecticut River in western New Hampshire. Most people know of the town because Dartmouth University was, and still is, located there.

Almy met his employer's 24-year-old blond-haired, blue-eyed daughter, Christine, while working on the Warden farm. Contemporary sources described Christine as being "of fine, rounded form and discreet manners." She was an active woman, always doing something for the Grafton Star Grange, or the New Hampshire College of Agriculture, or helping on her father's farm. The farmer's daughter was immediately attracted to the mysterious new farmhand, and Frank Almy was immediately attracted to her.

Fanny Warden, Christine's 16-year-old sister, was immediately repulsed by Mr. Almy. She hated him the moment he came to farm, or so the newspapers would later state. After the murder it was said that Fanny was a shrewd judge of character and saw Almy/Abbott for the scoundrel he was.

These were naive times. Most people did not delve too deeply into their neighbor's psychological motives. There were plausible alternative explanations for Fanny's hatred of the newcomer other than what was subsequently reported in the newspapers. It was possible that Fanny felt threatened by the handsome Almy, a stranger who could marry Christine and break up her family. Maybe she wanted him herself and was jealous. Maybe she felt an intense rivalry for the newcomer's affections and knew he didn't care for childish teenagers. Maybe Fanny was not quite the good girl that everyone believed she was, and she saw her own undesirable characteristics mirrored in someone else, hating the other person for having them.

The couple spent a lot of time together. They went to church, washed dishes, danced at social functions, went on sleigh rides and read books together, although Christine was constantly trying to improve Almy's taste in literature. They did not live together, nor as far anyone knows did they have sex. Their relationship was said to be platonic. It was an old-fashioned courtship.

No matter what the couple may have felt for one another, no matter how much pain it may eventually cause her older sister, Fanny was determined to see the relationship end. Every time an opportunity presented itself she would pass a poisonous remark. Frank was always the target of her toxic barbs. He could do nothing right and his motives were always suspect. Eventually the poison took hold, and on

April 1, 1891, Andrew Walden fired Almy.

The overly critical believed that some people will never change. Many point to several angry outbursts as the reason for Almy's dismissal. Some have speculated Walden was afraid Christine would actually marry his hired hand, a man who did not come from a good family, and that would not do in Hanover. He didn't know about Almy's real background, at least Abbott came from a distinguished lineage.

As far as anyone knows, when Abbott became Frank Almy he left his life of crime behind. There were no waves of burglaries in Hanover while Almy worked on Warden's farm. There were no new crime waves anywhere he traveled after his escape. Like Dr. Jekyll and Mr. Hyde, there seemed to be two personalities at work, and the better one enjoyed brief victory.

Christine cried the day Almy left and Fanny was overjoyed. Whatever symbolic meaning her victory had would later be compounded by tragedy, but she would always be able say, "I told you so."

Frank traveled around New England for the next two months, picking up his stored belongings from several boarding houses. At one of them he showed the landlady a picture of Christine and sadly said, "If I don't have her, then no other fellow will, either." Something deep inside Almy/Abbott was snapping, some part of his character was regressing, and he was about to become Abbott again.

On June 13 the final break occurred. Abbott took a train from Boston to White River Junction, Vermont, from the station he walked to Hanover, and from Hanover to a small town called Norwich. Keeping to the back roads, he made his way to the Warden farm. No one saw him because he arrived close to midnight.

Like an apparition mingling with the shadows, Abbott prowled the grounds around the house for an hour, while the Wardens were soundly asleep inside. Then, as if following instructions from an inner demon, he went into the barn and built himself a roomy cave in the hay.

He lived in his hay cave for a little more than a month, 20 yards from his beloved. At night he roamed the countryside gathering food and visiting the places where Christine might be found to no avail. He did rudely awaken a few Hanover residents during his nightly sojourns. They were so shocked at seeing this shadow move across their rooms that they let it slip back into the night undisturbed. Abbott also visited the Warden house on a few occasions, caressing the piano keys that Christine used to play for him.

On July 17 his twilight existence came to an end. While Abbott was hiding in his hay cave he over-

Prisons in Abbott's day dealt out extreme forms of punishment as matter of routine.

Windsor Prison, Vermont where young Abbott was sentenced for 15 years. It was the most escape-proof prison in New England. Six years later Abbott busted out Windsor and became a local legend.

heard the Wardens outside discussing a Grange meeting scheduled for that evening. The whole family was going. Here was Abbott's chance to see Christine again; he was overjoyed. But that evening she wasn't alone when she walked to the meeting hall. Christine was surrounded by her mother, a neighbor and the hateful Fanny. Keeping at a safe distance, Abbott followed the Warden family to the Grange. While the meeting was in progress he stayed hidden among the trees.

No one can know what was going on in Abbott's mind while he waited for the Grange meeting to finish. Had he seen Christine on the way to the meeting perhaps everything might have ended differently. When the meeting ended the four women walked back to the Warden house. Their stroll took the group through an area known as the Vale of Tempe.

The Vale of Tempe was really a wooded glen with a small sparkling brook rushing through it. In the light of the almost full moon it had a fairy tale quality. The vale was separated from the road and the surrounding area by cedar fences. When Daniel Webster, class of 1801, was a student at Dartmouth, he used to practice his oratory skills in the Vale with the trees standing as a mute audience.

As the women approached the vale Abbott stepped out from the shadow of a large tree and said, "Mrs. Warden, you know me, I'm Frank Almy. I only want to talk to Christine." Under any other circumstances this abrupt encounter might have provoked a discussion about the propriety of such a request. But this man had a certain urgency about him. He had a revolver in his right hand and plain enough in the bright moonlight.

Mrs. Warden and her friend where frozen to the spot with terror. Abbott turned to Christine and took her arm saying, "I've come a thousand miles to meet you." Fanny was not as terrified as the adults.

She grabbed her sister's other arm and began to pull Christine away from Abbott. For a brief moment it looked as if two people were pulling a life-sized rag doll in opposite directions. Abbott was enraged by Fanny's interference. He pushed the barrel of the gun in the young girl's face. "Fan, I hate you," he said as his finger tightened on the trigger. "If you don't let go, I'll kill you." This must have scared Fanny, for she just stood there as Abbott yanked her older sister away from her grasp.

Abbott shoved Christine through the cedar fence and into the Vale. The still silent object of Abbott's affections fell down, and her boyfriend was forced to drag her along the ground by her feet. The dazed Fanny came back to her old self and chased after them. She climbed the fence and ran toward Abbott at full speed. A shot rang out and something whizzed past Fanny. A second shot was fired. This bullet must have had Fanny's name on it, for it would have hit her had she not either thrown herself to the ground or tripped on something in the dirt.

As Fanny lay there Mrs. Warden and her friend ran down the road screaming for help. A few moments passed, just long enough for the yells of the terrified women to mingle with the wind in the trees; just long enough to hear the sounds of two people scuffling off in the distance.

For a few breaths there was silence and then Fanny heard Christine cry out, "Help, Fan! He's tearing all my clothes off!" The younger sister was up like a shot, first running toward her sister and then back toward the road. Fanny found herself running back and forth in a rare moment of vacillation.

The road won the battle of indecision. As soon as she climbed over the cedar fence Fanny met a passing farmer attracted by Christine's shouts. Quickly she explained the situation. The farmer knew the Warden family and he was very decisive. He climbed the fence and made straight away for the area where Christine's shouts came from.

Two shots stopped the rescuers in their tracks. In between the two cracks Fanny and the farmer heard a loud and long desperate moan. Without regard for their safety, they ran toward the sounds. In the moonlight they caught a fleeting glimpse of Abbott vanishing into the woods.

Christine's body almost glowed in the moonlight. Only the dark patches of blood about the head and torso reminded the farmer and Fanny of the awful truth. Christine was dead. Her underwear was ripped off her and lay in tatters about the body. Her dress and petticoats were shredded and spread out in clumps about the Vale.

The police were called and Christine's body was examined at the site of the murder by one of Hanover's town doctors. He concluded that the first bullet crashed through the woman's head and the second bullet tore through her vagina, the latter bullet destroying any evidence of rape. In 1891 it was assumed that a proper woman would have remained a virgin until she was married. The doctor reasoned that her killer wanted to hide the fact that Christine's maidenhead was not still intact.

The residents of Hanover learned of the heinous crime shortly before midnight when the great bell in Dartmouth Hall tolled. No one remembered a crime like this ever being committed in the university town. Everyone was horrified and everyone wanted to get involved. Students, professors, tradesmen and merchants all banded together until their number had swollen to over 200. With a righteous purpose they set out to hunt for the fiend of the Vale.

Too bad they did not know whom they were really hunting. If anyone had the slightest inkling that it was George Abbott, notorious for his escape from Windsor Prison, and equally so for his hand carved treasure cave and string of daring burglaries, his hunters might have known where to look and what to look for. But they futilely kept searching for Frank Almy, and thus nothing was found of their quarry for over a month.

Abbott was never far away. He had returned to his hay cave and taken up permanent residence. While rewards were added to rewards and more and more men where chasing phantoms across the New Hampshire/Vermont countryside, Abbott was expanding his hay cave into a hay condominium. He had a lookout perch in the north corner facing the Warden house. He must have mutely watched the hearse leave the house and carry Christine to her final resting place. After his capture Abbott told the police that each night he would gather wild flowers and place them on Christine's grave, and then sit for a few sorrowful hours with his dead love.

Night was also the time Abbott foraged for food. Where he went and how much he stole no one knows. By this time he was a very good master burglar; he was so good that no one in the area ever noticed anything missing.

It was Mrs. Warden who initially discovered Abbott's secret. On the hot afternoon of August 18 Christine's mother was hunting for some missing chickens. She searched in the shade of the barn, avoiding the blistering sun. A wooden board covering a small hole in the large building's foundation caught her eye. She kicked the board away and peeked inside the hole. To her amazement she saw a dozen empty fish and meat cans as well as four empty fruit preserve jars. This was quite puzzling. She went home and told her husband about her odd discovery. He searched inside the barn with some neighbors. Another cache of empty tin cans and glass jars was uncovered in the hay. Knowing he was on to something really big, he went to town the next day and summoned H.C. Brown, the sheriff. After hearing about the unusual circumstances at the Warden farm it was agreed that the sheriff and a temporary deputy, Professor G. Whitcher, would stand watch over the barn that night and report if anything out of the ordinary occurred.

That night, as it had on the evening of the murder, a bright moon lit the countryside in a fantasy-like glow. The two police officers on rural stakeout perceived nothing unusual until sometime around 1:30 a.m. A ghostly figure of a man seemed to emerge from the wall of the barn. The specter made his way toward the watchers. Both the sheriff and his temporary deputy grew worried. Any moment they expected the thin creature would find them, shoot them, stab them, do whatever specters did when they discovered they were being watched. Much to their relief the man stopped 15 feet away, under an apple tree. He picked some apples, eating some and stuffing the rest in a sack. While the wretched creature was busy with his apple chores, the sheriff and the professor noticed that he was barefoot and dressed in rags, although they could not see his face clearly in the moonlight. When the man finished picking the apples, he walked back to the barn and appeared to vanish walking past the east corner.

News of this sighting spread like butter on a hot frying pan. Men from the surrounding towns came to join Sheriff Brown's posse. Everyone assumed the unknown man was Almy. The murderer had been free long enough. It was time to bring him to justice.

At dawn the 40 man posse struck. The plan was a simple one. The first posse would encircle the barn, then a select group of armed men would enter the building and begin searching for the fugitive. At 7:00 a.m. the posse secured the perimeter. A few minutes later a small party began searching the barn. They found nothing, not even a tin can. By 8:00 a.m. bells across the countryside, including the ones at Dartmouth Hall, sounded the call for more volunteers.

Several hundred men held an emergency meeting outside the barn. A couple of the more reckless members of the enlarged posse favored setting fire to the barn to flush out Almy. Warden reminded them that it was his barn and they would do no such thing. The posse went on to "Plan B" and sent another search party into the barn.

Charles Hewett, a summer student at Dartmouth, entered armed with a pitchfork and a revolver. To his left and right were 20 other members of the party slowly marching forward in a line, prodding the hay in front of them. Hewett was extra cautious, taking longer than his compatriots to examine the hay. His last pitchfork prod hit something odd, like a soft lump under the straw.

Suddenly the hay in front of the student flashed, a sharp crack resounded in the barn and Hewett saw the top of his knuckles fly way. Pop! Pop! The hay rose up. It briefly took the form of a scarecrow, then the straw fell away to reveal a ragged man with a gun. Hewett dropped his pitchfork, drew his own gun and ducked for cover. Bullets were zipping past him. The student jumped up from his hiding place and found Abbott standing 10 feet in front of him. In a quick exchange of gunshots Hewett emptied his revolver at the killer. Abbott fell back into the hay. Then, like one of the inhuman monsters depicted in the cinema, Abbott rose again and crept toward the student. Pop! A small piece of Hewett's nose disappeared in a blood-red cloud. Enough was enough! The student jumped through a hole in the floor to the ground. Another whizzing bullet followed him as he ran outside.

The indoor search party had scattered when they heard the gunfire. One man was searching the rafters when he found himself trapped on a ladder. He watched Hewett escape, turned around and took a shot at Abbott. The sniper missed and took a bullet in the shoulder for his effort. The volunteer fell off his perch to the barn floor. As wounds go it was minor, but he lay there still fearing for his life. More shots rang out from all over the barn. Bullets flew through the air, but none reached their targets. Smoky clouds of freshly ignited gunpowder created a thick haze. For a few moments no one was sure who was the killer and who were the hunters. The confused posse beat a hasty retreat carrying the wounded man with them.

By now over a thousand people had gathered by Warden's barn. Another small group of volunteers entered the barn, but this time Abbott, still known only as Almy, wanted to negotiate. From his hiding place he said he would give himself up, if the sheriff promised that he would not be lynched. To prove his sincerity Abbott threw out a stack of Christine's love letters. He told the volunteers the letters would give, "the written cause for the crime I committed."

At first a small vocal minority chanted "Hang him! Hang him!" They were probably the same people who voted to burn down the barn. Finally, after a brief discussion, calmer heads prevailed and Abbott was allowed to give himself up. When he staggered out of the barn the posse saw that he was wounded in the head and the left upper thigh. The head wound was a minor cut in the scalp. The thigh wound was serious enough to be treated at Wheelock's Hospital in Hanover.

While Almy was being treated at the hospital his true identity was discovered. No one knows who first recognized the fugitive, but it caused a shock wave of surprise and consternation throughout the area. Abbott was New England's most famous criminal at the time. Many believed that he would never be caught. He was a larger-than-life folk hero; he was the man who escaped from Windsor Prison!

Before his trial, New Hampshire police officials moved Abbott to a series of larger and more secure prisons, fearful that he would escape from any jail that was too small or too lax. They had no way of knowing that Abbott had no intention of escaping.

At his trial Abbott plead guilty to Christine's murder, but he cited extenuating circumstances. According to his testimony, Christine promised to marry him. He read portions of Christine's letters as proof of her intentions. It must be said that there was substantial latitude for various interpretations within the letters.

In one letter, that was later published in local newspapers, Christine admonishes Almy, "Since living with us you have not gained my highest regard... Your conduct at the card table has given me more insight into the dark side of character. I would never think of marrying a man to reform him." And at the end of the same letter Christine says, " Frank I shall test the strength of your love. Can you open your heart to all the good influences, practice rigid self-control and wait patiently? If it is ever so, I believe you will win in the end... I fear I am not worthy of such a love, but I cannot be satisfied unless the man I love is able to help me become better, for I am weak, rather than to drag me down." Somehow conclusions like this kept the flame of hope alive in Abbott's heart, and he truly expected to marry Christine someday.

But the final word and ending was written by Fanny. When she took the stand she nailed Abbott's coffin shut. Her venomous testimony about the murder and about Abbott's stay in the Warden home was all the jury needed to come to a verdict. He was found guilty. On March 16, 1892 George Abbott, alias Frank Almy, was hanged at Concord Prison.

1892
A Famous Chopper

Lizzie Borden took an axe,
Gave her mother forty whacks;
When she saw what she had done,
She gave her father forty-one.

The axe murder victims were Andrew Jackson Borden, 69, and his wife Abby (Grey) Borden, 65. There is little to say about Abby Borden. She was Andrew Borden's second wife; his first wife died when Lizzie was quite young. The second Mrs. Borden had a cordial and sometimes friendly relationship with her two stepchildren, Lizzie and Emma. Wealthy Andrew Borden is another matter; everyone had something to say about him.

Andrew Borden was considered a proper member of society. In 1892 his contemporaries saw him as hard working and temperately thrifty. By the standards of a century later he would be seen as a workaholic and somewhat of a miser. The president of several banks, he owned most of the high income producing real estate in Fall River, Massachusetts. Despite all his accumulated wealth, very little of his money ever saw the light of day. Their Victorian house was not in the affluent part of town, certainly not where a bank president and real estate mogul would have been expected to live. His house lacked gaslight, a bathtub and a library, material goods and status symbols of the day that were found in less wealthy homes.

Borden did provide for his daughters by purchasing land and setting up bank accounts with substantial amounts of cash in them. In his will he left almost everything to his daughters, and very little to his wife. Unlike Willie Loman in *Death of a Salesmen*, Borden was not well liked and he didn't care. What he had was respect, respect built, in no small way, on fear and loathing.

It is easy to say that bank presidents can, in the course of business, make enemies, but Borden collected them like postage stamps. One week before he was murdered Borden was visited by an unidentified man whom he argued with for close to an hour. Finally the shouting became too much for Borden and he kicked the man out of his house. Burglaries were

occurring with a frightening frequency at the Borden home. The last burglary was committed in broad daylight, an almost unheard of occurrence in the best of homes.

Andrew Borden was a very strict parent, and as a result the Borden sisters lived a very sheltered life. Lizzie, 32, and Emma, 41, were both well into spinsterhood. No one has ever mentioned either of them having been courted or dating. Perhaps their father preferred it that way.

On his last day alive Andrew Jackson Borden sat down to breakfast with his wife, and his daughter, Lizzie. His other daughter, Emma, was away visiting friends. It was a hot August morning, but Borden insisted that all the windows in the room be closed. They were served by their Irish immigrant maid, Bridget Sullivan. Unlike other wealthy households, Bridget was never treated as a member of the family and consequently never took her meals with the Bordens. Bridget considered herself lucky not to have to eat this day's breakfast. The meal consisted of week-old mutton, mutton soup, week-old pungent bananas, bread and coffee; waste not, want not, as Borden would say. In keeping with his philosophy he left the house at 9 a.m. sharp to collect rents.

The women went about their routines for the next hour and a half. Abby Borden was upstairs making up the guest room for an unknown amount of time. Bridget was outside cleaning the windows. Several neighbors had seen her working, but not for the entire hour and a half she claimed to have been cleaning the exterior of the house. Lizzie was inside the house doing little personal chores.

When Andrew Borden came home the front door was locked, and he had to be let in by Bridget who used the side door. At that time Andrew was informed by his daughter that Abby had gone out after receiving "a note from a sick friend." Bridget noticed that Lizzie was on the bottom steps of the main staircase and had been on her way to the second floor when her father entered.

From the time that Andrew Borden came home until 11:10 a.m., the family continued doing chores inside and outside of the house. Bridget finished

Fall River, Massachusetts would never enjoy such notoriety again as when Lizzie Borden's trial took place. Local entrepreneurs were quick to print postcards of such interesting sights as the town custom house and post office.

cleaning and went to her room for a nap, in the stifling attic. Lizzie finished her ironing and went outside to either gather some fishing sinkers or to eat some fresh pears from the tree. Andrew Borden settled in the sitting room and rested on the sofa. Sometime during this period Abby had returned to the homestead.

There seemed to be nothing else for the Borden household to do, except for Lizzie. She was about to discover that she was an orphan. Later some would say it really wasn't a discovery, she already knew.

Bridget's nap was cut short by Lizzie's frantic calls for help. "Come down, quick! Father's dead! Somebody came in and killed him!" The maid rushed downstairs and found Lizzie in a confused state. She was standing at the door to the sitting room. Lizzie

pleaded with Bridget not to go inside but to hurry and get Dr. Bowen instead. When it was learned that the doctor was out on a house call, the next few minutes became a confusing swirl of events. Poor Lizzie asked the maid to run here and there, to get this neighbor and that neighbor, to find this doctor and that doctor. If this was an act it was very, very good, for she truly seemed to be a person in shock.

By the time the police came, Dr. Bowen and several neighbors had arrived at the Borden house. Lizzie had already mentioned to various people that she was outside eating pears when it happened, and that she had come inside when she heard a groan. Lizzie also said she was in the barn looking for fishing sinkers.

Nothing can prepare someone for the sight of a

Not only did Lizzie Borden inspire nursery rhymes, but numerous plays, novels and movies as well. To this day no one has been able to answer the all important question, "Did she or didn't she?"

brutal murder. Dr. Bowen and the police walked into the sitting room and were greeted by the sight of Andrew Borden lying on the sofa with his face all but chopped away, and his skull bashed in. Splattered on and behind the sofa was an enormous quantity of Borden's blood, like a grotesque Jackson Pollack painting. The assault must have happened quickly for there was no sign of a struggle. Dr. Bowen noted that Andrew Borden's hands were not clenched, indicating that the victim did not even have time to protect himself. After examining the body Dr. Bowen turned quite pale, left the room on unsteady legs and became ill.

Meanwhile Lizzie was sitting in the kitchen, mumbling in anguish. Several neighbors had gathered around to comfort her. At one point someone asked Lizzie where her mother was. Lizzie's reply

must have brought a chill to the good women attending her. She told them in a flat, matter-of-fact voice, that her mother went out to visit a sick friend. She must have returned and been killed too.

Then she added that her father had enemies and because of this their milk had been poisoned. In all fairness to Lizzie, the family became violently ill after eating the preceding evening's dinner, and they may have believed that someone had tried to poison them. Unfortunately, this and certain other facts brought out during the trial, would come back to haunt the distraught woman.

Upon hearing this everyone rushed upstairs. There in the guest room, facing the wall with her rear in the air, prostrate as if in Islamic prayer, was Abby Borden with her skull crushed and her brains laid bare. Just as in the living room the wall in front of the dead woman was heavily speckled with blood.

The medical examiner counted the head gashes on both Mr. and Mrs. Borden. Abby Borden was the winner in this macabre lottery. She had 21 head wounds; her husband had only 11.

The police did not bother to check for fingerprints. In the turn of the century New England fingerprinting was considered un-American and therefore just not done. Law enforcement in the town of Fall River was also somewhat lax. The original list of blood stains was lost and before the trial it had to be rewritten from memory.

At first no one in this small protected New England town knew what to make of their worst crime of the century. While the citizens of Fall River went about bolting their doors, buying rifles and watching each other very carefully, the police and the town officials busied themselves with questioning Lizzie Borden as to her whereabouts at the time of the murder. The answers that the police received, as well as friends and relatives, were the same jumble of non sequiturs as on the day of the murders.

An inquest was held, but before the district attorney could decide on a course of action, Bridget Sullivan volunteered herself as a witness for the prosecution. Suspicion slowly surrounded Lizzie as innocuous circumstances took on ominous meanings in light of the murders.

A few days before the killings Lizzie had attempted to purchase hydrocyanic acid to clean a fur coat, but the pharmacist refused to sell it to her. Several experts testified that hydrocyanic acid was easily absorbed through the skin, deadly in small doses and hardly left a trace in those who were poisoned with it. Because of its toxicity, hydrocyanic acid was not used as a cleaning agent. This line of questioning led to the family's illness the night before the murders and Lizzie's rambling about the milk being poisoned. Furthermore, in the course of the investigation, it was discovered that a day before the murders Lizzie had bought a small axe. Since there were no other suspects and circumstantial evidence pointed to the spinster Borden woman, it seemed only right that Lizzie stand trial for murder.

The trial of Lizzie Borden attracted national attention because of her position in society. She was a 32-year-old spinster heiress, who devoted much of her time to the Woman's Christian Temperance Union and other such organizations. Lizzie Borden, a representative of old respectable New England stock, was on trial for brutally murdering her parents with an axe. Across the nation many found it unbelievable that a lady could commit such a shocking crime. Coverage of the trial was guaranteed to sell newspapers.

Ten months after Andrew and Abby Borden were killed, their daughter was fighting for her life in a Fall River courtroom. Initially some of the inquest findings were thrown out by the judge. This was an axe murder trial and all the suppositions about poisoning and attempting to purchase hydrocyanic acid were ruled irrelevant because they did not contribute to the cause of death.

The prosecution began with establishing Lizzie's motive—money. Both sisters were going to be disinherited by Mr. Borden in favor of his wife. The Borden daughters knew this and it was Lizzie who decided to act before her father's will could be changed. There was actually no factual basis for this line of reasoning, but it was the only motive the district attorney could think of. The prosecutor's real case rested on Lizzie's erratic behavior.

Where was the ubiquitous Lizzie Borden at the time of the murders? Where was the note from her mother's sick friend? Why doesn't her mother's sick friend come forward? Why can't she remember if she was eating pears or in the barn at the time of the murders? Pointing to Lizzie's flimsy answers concerning her whereabouts before and during the trial, the prosecution was beginning to think the case could be won.

A neighbor testified that a few days after the murders, she saw Lizzie burn a dress similar to the one she was wearing on the day of the killings. An axe was produced that was found under a pile of ashes in the Borden's cellar; the shape and size of the blade fit the wounds exactly. And Bridget, the maid, was the prosecution's star witness, always ready to substantiate the district attorney's assumptions.

For the defense Lizzie had several lawyers, one of whom was a popular ex-governor of Massachusetts, George D. Robinson. Quickly the axe from the cellar was discredited as a murder weapon. It had rust, not blood stains on it. Any number of Borden axes could have caused the same wounds. Lizzie and her sister both had substantial amounts of money without the inheritance. It was impossible to murder someone with an axe and not get splattered with blood yourself. This point was graphically demonstrated in the courtroom by Robinson. There was no time for Lizzie to change her clothes and wash. Police reports verified that the washroom and basin were dry when they arrived. Neighbors corroborated the defense statement that Lizzie was wearing the same spotlessly clean dress after the murders as she was seen wearing earlier that morning. Robinson made Bridget verify, under oath, that the dress Lizzie burned had paint on it, not blood. At the end of his summation Robinson said, "... To find Lizzie Borden guilty you must believe she is a fiend. Does she look it? She is a lady, and a Christian woman, the equal of your wife and mine."

After a 15-day trial and a jury deliberation of 90 minutes, Lizzie Borden was found not guilty. The courtroom, filled with spectators from Lizzie's church and social clubs, broke into applause.

After the trial life was never the same for the sisters. With their inheritance they moved to the best section of town. Lizzie was able to grow and enjoy her new found freedom. Although she never married, she threw herself into a life of social clubs. Emma could not adjust to her sister's new life style and left River Falls 12 years later. Many in town were surprised at Lizzie's investment acumen. Some of Andrew Borden, the old bank president, was in Lizzie. At her death the family fortune had grown close to a million dollars. In her will she left the sum of $30,000 to the Animal Rescue League.

Did she do it? No one will ever know for sure one way or another. A motive not discussed at the time was Andrew Borden's unenlightened ideas of child rearing. During his time he was seen as just a little strict with his daughters. Today, he would be considered a possessive monster, if not a child abuser. One can imagine attempting to date either of the Borden girls with Andrew Borden looking on. He made life extremely difficult for any possible suitors. Lizzie may have decided that she had enough and in a unpremeditated frenzy cut herself free from her father's intolerable bonds. In a similar murder case in the 1920s, it was shown that a murderer doesn't have to get him or herself splattered with blood when killing someone with an axe.

One person whom the prosecution implied could have killed the Bordens was Emma. A popular theory surfaced in the 20s that the elder daughter came back to the house from Fairhaven, 15 miles away, killed her parents and returned to her friends before anyone knew that she was gone. Her motive also may have been her father's possessiveness.

In some mystery fictions the butler really does do it. In the Borden case it very well could have been the maid. Bridget Sullivan was unhappy in the Borden household. She had complained to her friends that she was never part of the Borden family. In fact, both Andrew and Abby constantly went out of their way to point this out to the maid. She was never allowed in the bedrooms on the second floor. She was never allowed to eat with the family. She was shrewdly paid just enough money for her to live on, but never enough to allow her to leave the Borden's employment. She was more of a slave than a servant. It is not difficult to imagine all her pent up animosity bursting forth in an axe wielding rage. Let us not forget that Bridget was very enthusiastic about being the prosecution's star witness.

But this is all conjecture. Until someone uncovers a lost letter or a misplaced statement, we will never be sure whether or not Lizzie Borden deserves to be the central character of a morbid children's nursery rhyme. Till this day the question remains, "Did she or didn't she?"

1922
In Those Silent Days

In 1894 the first movie studio was born in West Orange, New Jersey. It was Thomas Edison's Kinetograph Studios, housed in a black building known as the "Black Maria." In the era before studio lights, the black clad building rotated on tracks that followed the sun. The early films produced at Kinetograph were nothing more than a continuous 47-foot film loop which ran on spools between an incandescent lamp and a shutter to simulate motion between the still frames. All this was housed in a hand-driven, coin-operated, peepshow device. Its mechanical simplicity was the heart of today's modern film projector without a motor.

Within 14 short years motion pictures became a glamorous, growing industry. Millions of people entered darkened rooms and watched silent stories projected on large screens, sometimes accompanied by live piano music. The faces of many actors and actresses became as well known to the audience as the faces of some of their neighbors.

In 1911 many east coast studios moved to a small industrial town in California to escape some of Edison's industry wide restrictive business practices. The town was named Hollywood and soon Hollywood would become synonymous with everything that is glamorous in American cinema.

So powerful was, and is, America's interest in Hollywood that in 1922 most of the nation chose to ignore the sensational Hall-Mills, New Jersey murders, and the resultant "Million Dollar Trial." Instead, the public chose to read about the untimely death of William Desmond Taylor, a Hollywood director. "Whodunit" is still being debated today.

Adolph Zukor, head of Paramount Studios, thought William Desmond Taylor was one of the greatest silent film directors of his time. Of course, Zukor's judgment may have been clouded by the fact that Taylor worked for Famous Players Lasky Studios, a profitable division of Paramount.

Zukor always had the feeling that being the head of a movie studio could be compared to sitting on top of a volcano. Every so often something happens below that causes the whole thing to erupt. These fiery events come in the form of periodic scandals which occur because Hollywood is a tight-knit artistic community, and as so often happens, certain members indulge their whims to excess. Taylor was no exception; his spare time exploits even shocked members of the land of celluloid make-believe.

When it came to sexual prowess Taylor was rumored to be an athlete. Starlets and stars beat a path to his bed. Some were looking to advance their careers and some wanted to enjoy the pleasures of his legendary techniques. Taylor was known to have as many as three or four different sexual encounters in one night; some of those nights it was three or four participants at the same time. Many famous female leads were sexually linked to Taylor. Among them were silent screen stars Mabel Normand, the Max Sennett comedienne, and Mary Miles Minter.

But this was Hollywood and all that meets the eye is not as it appears. There are those who say that Taylor's insatiable image was manufactured by the studio heads to hide an even more scandalous truth. Taylor was a self-made man. What money he had, he earned by making movies. He was one of the wealthiest directors of his day. Unlike many other inhabitants of the nascent tinsel town, he read books, collected real works of art and had a fine eye for expensive antiques.

Taylor was tall and, due to his distinctive well bred English accent, seemed very British. During World War I he left Hollywood in 1917 to fight in the Royal Canadian army. He returned in 1919 a captain, an accomplishment of which he was inordinately proud.

Prior to his film career, the noted film director's past was shrouded in attractive mystery. Not much was known about the dashing director before Hollywood, yet everyone wanted to hold on to their romantic notions about him. Everyone had their reasons to leave his past unknown. According to the official studio biographies, Taylor appeared out of nowhere in 1910 acting in bit parts. By 1914 he was a lead player. In less than a year he made the transition to director with all due speed and ease. On the night of February 1, 1922, Taylor was at the height of his career. There seem to be no doubt that he was well on his way to becoming a silent film legend when death stepped in and changed the script.

The evening started out as a typical night in the Taylor mansion. Mabel Normand stopped by to pick up some books. Choosing and lending books was part of the director's education campaign for his lovers of long standing, and Normand was in need of a change in direction. Tayor's interest was one of a rescue mission, coupled with an occasional nightly union, to keep things in proper perspective.

Although it was not apparent at the time, Mabel Normand was approaching the final downward slide of her film career. She started out as many young actresses do, as a model. While modeling on a film set near New York City, she met D.W. Griffith's associate, Mack Sennett. Against her parents' wishes she signed acting contracts with Biograph and Vitagraph studios, two of the major film companies of the day. In 1910 almost all American film production was still being shot in the New York area. When Griffith moved to California, to get away from Edison's overbearing control, he dropped Normand's contract. She didn't stay unemployed long. Sennett became romantically involved with Mabel and she soon moved to Hollywood, where she was given a contract with her lover's Keystone Studios. Here she was in close contact with co-workers Gloria Swanson, W.C. Fields and Charlie Chaplin.

Several days before she was to marry Sennett, Mabel found her fiancé in bed with another actress. Rather than shriek and run for cover the actress attacked Mabel with a vase, knocking her out. Sennett unceremoniously dumped her unconscious body on Fatty Arbuckle's porch.

Although she and Sennett soon patched things up, the wedding was called off. Within the year she had signed a new contract with Samuel Goldwyn. By now she was rumored to be taking drugs, specifically cocaine, and her professional behavior was becoming erratic at best. She still continued to be a hit with the critics and movie-goers alike, but by 1921 her popularity was waning and Mack Sennett was one of the few producers who would hire her.

On this fateful night Normand was greeted by Henry Peavey, Taylor's effeminate and reputedly homosexual butler, and shown into the large living room. The director, with the large sexual appetite, was in his study, having an argument over the telephone with someone. At times the conversation was quite heated. Because of the distance between the study and the living room, the words were indistinct and Mabel couldn't make out the subject. Taylor hung up the phone and kissed Mabel after coming into the living room. Mabel let it be known that she was not staying the night because she was already

very tired. He gave her several carefully selected books by Freud and Nietzsche.

Peavey was given the rest of the night off and he left the house at 7:15 p.m. Taylor spent the next half hour complaining about his former butler, Edward F. Sands, who had stolen jewelry, forged his checks, charged large sums to his accounts and smashed up one of his cars. All of this larceny and vandalism was done while the director was in Europe. When Taylor returned, Sands was gone. Even after Sands had disappeared there were several more burglaries, and more forged checks were cashed. He showed Mabel two forged checks. Normand commented that the forgeries were very good indeed, as if someone who had known Taylor a long time had done them. He made an odd face at her statement.

At 7:45 p.m. Mabel said good-bye and left the house. At 8:15 p.m. a loud crack was heard in the vicinity of the Taylor's mansion. None of the neighbors thought it was anything more than a car backfiring. Unlike today's well tuned, computer chip regulated cars, the primitive automotive systems of the 1920s backfired quite often. Around 10:00 p.m. a neighbor noticed the lights were still on at Taylor's mansion, and he stopped by to say hello. Taylor did not answer the door. This was not unusual when the director was engaged in his favorite horizontal activities. The neighbor left. A half an hour later his chauffeur returned the car, knocked on the door, received no answer and left imagining the bawdy action in the mansion.

Arriving at his usual time the next day, 7:30 a.m., the butler started his duties. He began Taylor's breakfast, and while the coffee was brewing he went on to tidy up the living room. What he saw on the floor next to the desk was to abruptly change his life forever. Stiffly lying on the rug with his arms at his side was William Desmond Taylor, looking like a toppled wooden soldier. From his mouth ran a rivulet of crimson dried blood. On top of the body was an overturned chair. There was no doubt the former Royal Canadian army captain was very dead.

With a sound more like a police siren than a voice, Peavey ran screaming from the house. Outside he started to yell that Taylor was dead. He was to continue running though the streets yelling his head off for a half an hour. Later people would say the shock of that morning drove the poor man insane. His madness was permanent and he was committed to an insane asylum where he died in 1931. However, another version states he went into hiding from unnamed individuals, fearful they would kill him if he told anyone what he knew about some terrible secret. This account ends with Peavey dying impoverished and alone in 1937.

Mrs. Edward L. C. Robbins and her daughter Ethel Daisy Dean
Tanner seen in photo taken shortly after Taylor's murder. They
were the director's abandoned wife and daughter. When Ethel May
Harrison met Taylor in New York he was known as William Tanner. They were married 1901 and later had daughter named Daisy.
After 7 years of marriage he left them and for parts unknown. Years
later she saw her missing husband acting in a movie. One can only
imagine her surprise.

Neighbors who first heard the news called Mabel Normand, who in turn called the studio, who in turn notified Adolph Zukor of the news, who in turn sent some of his executives to the house. Zukor arrived shortly after. As word spread many other studio chiefs converged on the Taylor mansion.

A doctor was found in the neighborhood and brought to the house. He took one quick look at the body and pronounced that Taylor died of a gastric hemorrhage. Having given his diagnosis from the hip, he promptly left.

The Taylor mansion seemed like a gathering of the studio gods around a fallen hero. They were milling around the body and trying to figure out what they should do next when Adolph Zukor breezed in. One glance at the body was all it took for Zukor to tell his employees to search and destroy anything that could hurt the studio's reputation. Instantly the executives raced through the house gathering up love letters, miscellaneous papers and all of Taylor's booze. Possessing liquor in those days was at the very least a social taboo. Three years before Congress had passed an amendment banishing alcohol, and even Hollywood had to give the appearance of abiding with the new prohibition laws. Everything that had writing on it was inspected. Any paper that were found to be the least bit suspicious were thrown into the fireplace and a fire was started.

Mabel Normand arrived. She was scarcely noticed as she raced upstairs to the bedroom in search of her love letters. Meanwhile the butler was still running around the neighborhood screaming that Taylor was dead. Finally someone called the police to get the man to stop making all that racket.

Finally the forces of law and order arrived on the scene. For about a minute they were barely noticed. Then, one by one the police restrained the studio executives from committing any further acts of self-serving vandalism. It was the assistant coroner's examination of the victim that forced the tinsel town titans to finally pay attention to Taylor's body. While the examination was in progress, one of the studio executives suggested the coroner turn the body over. There, to everyone's shock, were two bullet holes. Taylor didn't die of natural causes, he was murdered! Murder was a hotter topic than the peaceful death of a lecherous director. That news made the rounds even faster than the news of Taylor's death.

Mary Miles Minter heard the news from her mother. At the time Minter was as famous as Mary Pickford. On screen she looked like a teenager, and to the press she was about 20 years old, yet her birth certificate said she was 30. Each film she made with Taylor increased his popularity with the audience, but for some unknown reason Minter's went down.

Mary Miles Minter was born Juliet Shelby in 1902. Her impulsive mother, Charlotte Shelby, the former Lily Pearl Miles of Shreveport, Louisiana, had on again-off again affairs with several husbands and the theater. When she saw Juliet's theatrical career outshine both herself and her oldest daughter, she didn't get mad ...she cashed in. When legal problems arose with regard to the child labor laws, the 11-year-old Juliet became a 16-year-old Mary Miles Minter. This was a shrewd fraud engineered by her mother, who appropriated her dead niece's name and birth certificate.

In 1915 Charlotte realized there was more money in movies, always hungry for beautiful young actresses, than on the stage. Shelby began a whirlwind campaign to find a studio for her talented daughter, and in no time Mary was signed to a six picture deal with Metro Pictures. Charlotte Shelby became the archetype by which all other stage-mothers are measured. She managed Mary's career and it reached incredible peaks. The highlight came when Shelby gathered a small army of lawyers to legally break Mary's contract with one studio so her daughter could sign with Paramount for $1,300,000. Mother and daughter had reached the pinnacle of Hollywood's starry heights. But in 1922 the family success was well into its twilight.

Not too many people knew of her affair with Taylor. Her mother knew and did not approve of the director. His rakish reputation gave the woman anxiety attacks when she thought of her daughter spending time with him.

Mary had recently broken away from her mother's control and was living at her grandmother's house. This was not the first time her grandmother had taken Minter under her wing. When Mary saw her mother approaching she locked herself in her room. Her mother shouted word of Taylor's death through the bolted door. Shelby demanded to know where her daughter was last night. Shocked, Mary unbolted the door and raced past her mother. Charlotte's visit was a poor attempt in stopping the actress from going to the Taylor mansion. She accomplished the exact opposite.

The police did not allow Mary into the mansion. Mary pleaded and began to weep, it was a better performance than any she did on the screen. The uniformed audience was unaffected by her show of emotion; too many people had wandered through the house already. Minter left the mansion and went to Mabel Normand's house. She stayed there until dark. No one knows what they said to each other for those hours, but they had a common bond in the man they loved and the letters they could not find.

What the actresses did not recover the police

found. Some of Normand's letters were found in Taylor's boots. Some of Mary Miles Minter's letters were so well hidden they were found days later. Some of the letters found their way to newspapers. Those who read them in the tabloids agreed that the Minter/Normand love notes were hot stuff. What Zukor hoped to avoid happened anyway. Normand's letters became known as the Blessed Baby Letters, for she signed every one of them "Blessed Baby."

Taylor's death caused ever-widening ripples of scandal to wash over the movie colony. Mary Pickford's name was included in the gossip for a time as one of Taylor's fun-loving night callers. There was no truth in that rumor, yet it made the rounds.

Investigators uncovered what few real clues to the murder remained after the studio executives' scavenger hunt. Cigarette butts were discovered outside the kitchen door, indicating someone may have waited there until the director was alone. Taylor was killed at close range with a .38 caliber pistol. The alignment of the bullet holes with the jacket and wounds proved that the director was shot in the back while sitting at his desk. One of the neighbors reported to the police that he saw someone dressed as a man, but with a distinctly feminine walk, leave

the Taylor house just after the "backfire." Beyond those paltry findings the police had little to go on.

Lacking clues, the investigators theorized that perhaps someone or something in William Desmond Taylor's past may have led to his murder. They began the arduous task of tracking down Taylor's pre-Hollywood life. In this they were successful.

The man behind William Desmond Taylor was an Irishman named William Cunningham Deane Tanner from County Cork. He was born the eldest son of a wealthy family in 1877. Instead of following the family tradition in military service, Deane Tanner joined a theatrical company after he graduated from Oxford in 1895. Although Taylor thought the theater was in his blood, the company did not want him in theirs. He left and traveled to the New World.

For a while he and his younger brother, Dennis, worked on a ranch in Harper, Kansas. Soon afterwards the brothers came to New York and started a successful antique shop. The money for the enterprise was borrowed from members of the New York upper crust, who readily took a liking to the charming "English" gentleman. He married the actress Ethel May Harrison in 1901 and moved to Larchmont. Rumors circulating in the best of New

William Desmond Taylor had everything going for him at the time this picture was taken. Little did he realize that in a few short months his complex social life would cause his violent death.

York circles stated that Taylor lived above his means and in turn his brother had to do with drawing less than an equal share of the business. There was no doubt the elder brother always lived in high style. Another explanation for Taylor's flamboyant life style was his heavy borrowing from his wife's uncle, the real estate magnate Daniel J. Braker. If this was true he never bothered to pay back what he owed.

No one knows exactly what happened in October 1908, but whatever occurred changed Taylor's whole life. He left his wife, his young daughter, Daisy, his brother and his business from which the stole $500. It was all rather sudden. A few days later he was seen quite drunk at the Vanderbilt Cup Race, and then he disappeared.

Taylor aimlessly wandered about the United States and Canada for five years. It is known that he worked alternately as a hotel manager, prospector and a mine timekeeper during his travels. After he disappeared his wife obtained a divorce from Taylor. His younger brother, unable to run the antique shop on his own, deserted the business and his wife, too.

Both of the Taylor wives found out that their spouses were still alive by accidentally seeing them acting on the silver screen. Needless to say, both wives were rather shocked. Only Dennis Tanner's wife made the trip to Hollywood to track down her husband. When she met with Taylor, his directorial star was rising. He could not or would not tell her the whereabouts of her errant husband, but he did send the woman some money each month for her daughter's education.

From this historical research the police concluded that the thieving butler, Edward Sands, was none other than Taylor's younger brother, Dennis. This was never fully proven but for a while he became a prime suspect in the murder. Edward Sands was never found, and there are those who believed that he murdered Taylor for running out on the lucrative antique business in New York.

Drugs, the illicit American pastime of the latter part of the 20th century, may have played a part in Taylor and Mabel Normand's lives, too. There are several different versions to the story. One states that the two lovers would regularly partake in opium parties. They would buy the drug in Chinatown and later smoke the sticky substance with friends in Taylor's house. Another version has Taylor and Normand using the drug alone. Some believed that opium was only Mabel Normand's vice. Taylor thought it was a filthy habit and did his best to make her quit. No matter which story was told the outcome was always the same—a drug dealer killed Taylor to protect himself.

Recently a new wrinkle has been added to the drug dealer theory. Writer Robert Giroux has written a book, *A Deed of Death*, which speculates that drug dealers hired a professional hit-man to get rid of Taylor. The drug associated in this version was cocaine, not opium, and Mabel Normand may have been involved with the dealer.

Part of this notion rests on a foundation of peanuts. It turns out that Normand was seen eating from a bag of peanuts when she left Taylor's mansion. A very strong and persistent rumor had it that Mabel's boyfriend and cocaine supplier held a legitimate job as a peanut vendor. There was a small panic, at that time, over a rumor of Taylor's intentions to begin a campaign to clean Hollywood of drugs. He was killed to keep him quiet.

Now if this theory hasn't muddied the waters there is another supposition, Taylor was not the ladies man everyone thought he was. He was gay. According to silent film star Claire Windsor, not one woman she knew ever slept with Taylor. She had known the fabulous director and seen him leave some of Hollywood's more glittering parties in the company of other men.

It was also true that on the day his body was found, Taylor was scheduled to testify on behalf of Henry Peavey. Peavey had been arrested several months earlier for soliciting young boys in a park.

Author and filmmaker Sidney Kirkpatrick, in the course of writing a biography on the noted film director King Vidor, came across an astonishing discovery. Many believe he may have come the closest to solving the mystery. Locked away in Vidor's private papers was a solution to the mystery that evaded trained detectives for 60 years. Vidor was fascinated with the Taylor murder; he wanted to do a movie about it. In 1967 he began his own investigation of the crime and may have uncovered the killer in the process.

The possible solution pins the murder on Mary Miles Minter's mother, Charlotte Shelby. She was a strong woman who would let nothing come between her and her control of Mary. The young actress was more than a daughter to Shelby, she was her livelihood. Mary's mother was also her manager. Her fee was an above standard 30 percent of earnings. Taylor had a very strong personality and became Shelby's rival for her daughter's affections. On the night of the murder it was Shelby who was seen dressed as a man walking with a feminine gait away from the Taylor house. Shelby got away with the murder by paying off one of the chief investigators. Mary Minter's life was destroyed by her mother's overprotectiveness, if not her self-interest. Her last

Almost ageless in appearance, Mary Miles Minter often played roles of women fifteen years younger. Her biggest part may have been off-screen as William Desmond Taylor's lover.

words to King Vidor were, "My mother killed every-thing I loved."

The only problem with the solution, so excitingly written in Kirkpatrick's book, *A Cast of Killers*, is the circumstantial and hearsay nature of the evidence. There was only a 50/50 chance of Charlotte Shelby being convicted in a jury trial on such evidence.

Many of the lives touched by the William Desmond Taylor murder were ruined by subsequent publicity. Although it was never proven that Mabel Normand was a drug addict, her career began to tumble. In 1923 she was involved in another violent incident. This time her chauffeur shot an oil tycoon who was dating her at the time. It was said that they were both in love with Mabel, but the chauffeur knew he could not compete with the millionaire, so he decided to rid himself of his rival. Fans quickly turned against Normand, and Max Sennett was forced to drop her as his leading comedienne. In 1930 she died, a broken woman, of tuberculosis.

In 1984, Mary Miles Minter died in obscurity. Her career was all but ended by the murder. Her life after Hollywood and stardom was one of litigation, successfully fighting her mother's bid, as her former manager, for part of her estate and also suing for libel those who included her as a suspect in the Taylor murder. Bitterness was her constant companion for the rest of her life.

Charlotte Shelby was reported to have died at least twice. The first time was in 1957, and later it was under an assumed name. Never did she say anything more about the murder than: "Why would anyone wish to shoot such a man?"

1924
A Couple of Bright and Murderous Guys: Leopold and Loeb

Nathan F. Leopold and Richard A. Loeb were wealthy and brilliant. Leopold had graduated from the University of Chicago at 18; Loeb from the University of Michigan at 17. The close friends were so smart that they had driven themselves into a profound state of boredom. They did not want for material objects and comforts, because they had more than enough money to buy almost anything. As for immaterial pleasures and pursuits, the two young men had either extensively read, discussed or explored them in great detail. There was no doubt in the pair's minds that they were certainly superior human beings. Part of the shared delusion came from their study of Nietzsche.

Friedrich Nietzsche was a 19th century German writer and philosopher and one of the most influential modern thinkers. His exploration of the root motives that underlie traditional Western civilization, particularly the triumph of the Enlightenment's secularism, was expressed in his observation that "God is dead." His approach to these ideas influenced the European intellectual agenda for decades after his death in 1900.

An ardent enemy of anti-Semitism, nationalism and power politics, his philosophy was perverted by early 20th century Fascists to advance the very things he hated. Much of this misunderstanding was caused by his sister, Elisabeth. Upon Nietzsche's death she obtained the rights to his literary works, and ruthlessly edited them for publication with no regard for their real meaning. It wasn't until 1908 and the publication of *Ecce Homo* that the European intellectual world had any indication of Nietzsche's true intent.

But this was 1924 and Fascism was on the rise throughout the world. Leopold and Loeb were particularly attracted to their own misunderstanding of the concept of the Nietzschean "Superman." Leopold devised a theory that Loeb could easily evolve into such a Superman, and when he did Leopold would become his chief acolyte. All this was rather strange. But when you are young, rich, bright and a Nietzschean Superman you certainly cannot be held to the mundane moral standards of right and wrong. Add to this list of favorable circumstances a large measure of boredom and something nasty will eventually occur.

At first Leopold and Loeb attempted to alleviate their malaise by committing petty crimes and arson. But that remedy only worked for a short time. Soon they were bored again and needed a bigger challenge. Nothing short of murder would do. It couldn't be any murder, it had to be the "perfect murder." Could a Superman accept anything less?

All types of potential victims were debated. Their respective fathers were rejected as candidates. Patricide and the huge inheritance involved would cast suspicion directly upon them. With all the unwanted attention the duo would receive, the murder could not be considered perfect. After eliminating everyone else they knew it came down to killing any victim, either known or unknown, selected at random.

Leopold and Loeb made extensive preparations before their victim was chosen. First and foremost they needed an automobile. This meant it had to be a rented car because the auto must not be linked to them or their families in any way. Automobile rentals were not common in 1924; in fact autos were not the familiar items that they are today. It was rare for anyone to own even one car, let alone two or three. Yet the Leopold and Loeb families had garages with several automobiles in each.

To facilitate the auto rental, and still leave an untraceable trail, they invented a phony identity.

Dear Sir:

Proceed immediately to the back platform of the train. Watch the east side of the track. Have your package ready. Look for the first LARGE, RED, BRICK factory situated immediately adjoining the tracks on the east. On top of this factory is a large, black watertower with the word CHAMPION written on it. Wait until you have COMPLETELY passed the south end of the factory - count five very rapidly and then IMMEDIATELY throw the package as far east as you can.

Remember that this is your only chance to recover your son.

Yours truly,

GEORGE JOHNSON

MR JACOB FRANKS

Should anyone else find this note, please leave it alone. The letter is very important.

The ransom note Leopold and Loeb sent to Jacob Franks. It was all planned so well, yet this note, designed to throw the police off the track, proved to be the killers' undoing.

Leopold accomplished this by staying in the Morrison Hotel in Chicago under the assumed name of Morton D. Ballard and opening a bank account in Ballard's name. Loeb was the man on the outside who sent mail and left phone messages for Mr. Ballard. When it came time to rent the car Mr. Ballard seemed to be what he said he was, a young sales representative who had business in the Chicago area.

The two men purchased some instruments for their forthcoming crime. According to the plan they needed a chisel to knock their victim unconscious, a rope to strangle him with, a large cloth to hide the body, a bottle of chloroform in case the chisel and rope did not work and a bottle of hydrochloric acid to mutilate the victim's features.

The same time they went on their shopping spree they wrote a ransom note demanding $10,000 in small, old bills. The victim's father would be told to put the money in a cigar box and wait for further instructions by telephone. Leopold named their fictitious abductor George Johnson. The teenage duo thought this was their pièce de résistance, camouflaging a cold-blooded murder as a kidnapping.

This note and the subsequent note to follow were typed on an Underwood typewriter that Leopold had stolen from the University of Chicago. Both murderers-to-be thought this was okay since they intended to dump the typewriter in some large body of water where it would never be found.

Now came the fun part, finding a victim. On the afternoon of May 21, 1924 Leopold and Loeb got in their rented car and went searching for a victim. They drove past an open field and watched some boys at play. It was in this crowd that the duo noticed a boy they knew named Levinson, but there was one big problem with this choice. There was no way they could keep a close watch on Levinson without showing themselves, and as fate would have it the killers forgot to bring Leopold's binoculars. So it was back to Leopold's house for his field glasses.

By the time Leopold and Loeb returned Levinson was gone. They searched the mob scene with the binoculars and found another victim, little 14-year-old Robert Franks. He was a friend of Loeb's younger brother and more importantly he had stopped playing and was walking toward his home. When Franks reached the street the killers pulled up along side of him, greeting the young teenager like a long lost buddy. "Come in a minute," Loeb said, exuding all of his senior teenage charm, "I want to ask you about a certain tennis racket." Loeb asked their victim if he minded if they took a detour before they drove him home. Poor little Robert must have been honored to have such smart and older guys take an interest in him. He said no, he didn't mind.

As Leopold stepped on the gas, the car shot forward. Simultaneously, with the rabbit-jump of the auto, Loeb whacked Franks' head with a chisel. The boy's body slumped and Loeb stuffed his mouth with a cloth. Franks died soon after the assault. This was the first change in Leopold and Loeb's plan. They expected to strangle their victim together. Each killer was to hold an end of the rope; Franks' neck would have been in the middle, and both teenagers would pull until the boy was dead. This maneuver would equally share the blame for his murder. Well, no matter, they thought, it was going to be the perfect crime anyway.

After the dead boy's body was covered with a large drop cloth, the killers rode around Chicago until a half an hour before sunset. At that time Leopold drove the car to a lakeside wetland south of the city, known as Hegewich. He was familiar with the area because he did most of his bird watching there. After stripping the body, Leopold and Loeb disfigured Franks with the acid and dumped his corpse in a railway culvert. They assumed Franks would be washed away with next rainfall, if not with the next high tide. Perfect murders need a lot of work to be successful. In the evening hours the killers were busy burying Franks shoes and belt, burning the rest of his clothing, hiding the chisel and finally mailing the ransom letter to Franks' father.

The next morning, just when they thought everything was ready for stage two of the perfect murder, the killers discovered that there was still one more chore to be done. The inconsiderate Franks had bled all over the back seat and floor of the rented car. Leopold and Loeb spent the morning cleaning up the blood with a mixture of water, detergent and kerosene. Leopold's chauffeur offered to help, but the murderous duo did a quick song and dance about how they had a hot time last night and had spilled some illegal red wine in car. They declined his offer and told the chauffeur it would be better if he did not involve himself with a minor violation of the Prohibition Laws.

After "Morton D. Ballard" returned the rented car, it was time for phase two, the ransom. Leopold called Mr. Franks and pretended to be George Johnson, the kidnapper who had Robert Franks in his custody. He demanded that the victim's father go to a certain drugstore where he would find a letter containing further instructions.

All this is quite extraordinary by our late 20th century expectations. The killers had posted the letter the night before and they were sure it would arrive at its destination by the next afternoon. Try doing that today.

MURDER

IN NORTH AMERICA
PORTFOLIO I

On the night of Helle Crafts'
murder, Richard Crafts claimed to
have been sitting in a diner,
drinking coffee for four hours,
while waiting for his shift as a
part time policeman at the Newtown police department to begin.
At first the Newtown police department would not believe that
Helle's disappearance was anything more than a family squab-
ble. They didn't even want to list
her as a missing person. Later
they would discover the truth
came in tiny bits and pieces.

The Silver Bridge where, on a cold and rainy night, Richard Crafts fed log sized chunks of his wife into an industrial sized woodchipper. Ground up portions of Helle Crafts emerged from the other end as tiny fragments which were spewed into the river below.

It was somewhere near this spot that Crafts was noticed by a fisherman grinding woodchips into the Housatonic River. He was incensed that anyone was would pollute the river in such an uncaring manner. The fisherman didn't know the half of it.

Joseph Hine, a roads department driver lead the police to the spot where he saw an unidentified man chip about a half a dozen wood-chip piles on the side of this road. It was in this area that Connecticut State Police recovered fragments of a blue cloth, some bone fragments, identified as belonging to the interior of a human skull, some tiny chopped up strands of blond hair and one dented dental crown. The latter would be positively identified as belonging to Helle Crafts.

Many serial killers stalk their victims long before they actually attack them. Some have been known to follow their victims for hours.

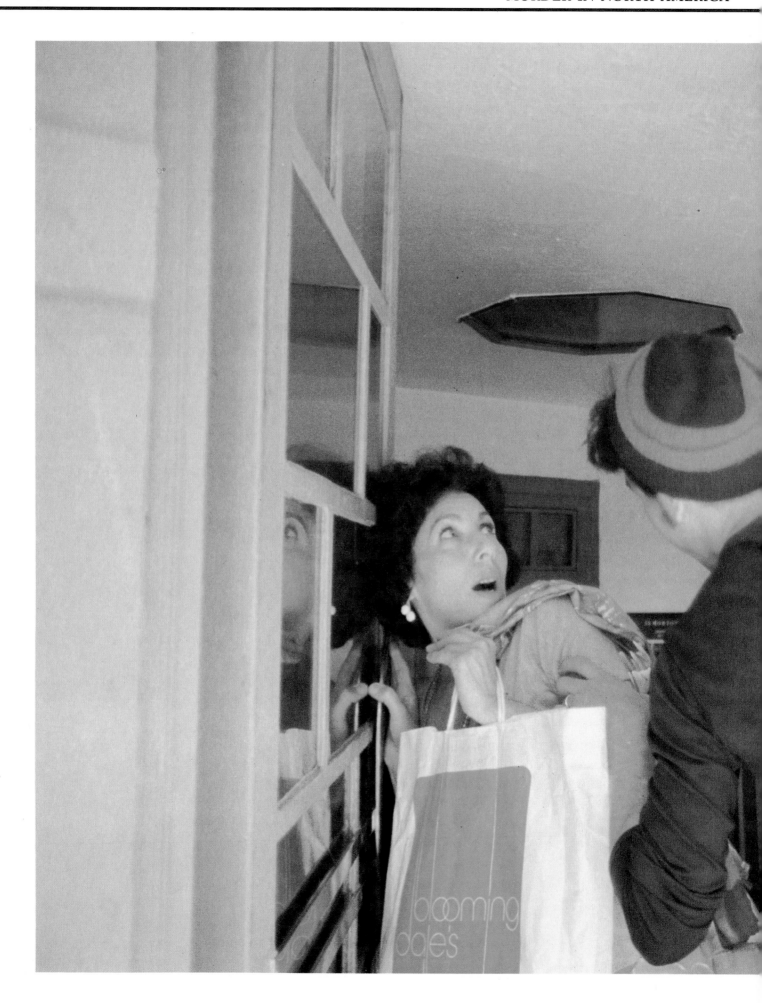

It is the fear of the unexpected random murder, like those homicides perpetrated by serial killers, that is most dreaded in our contemporary society.

Once a man entered Alcatraz he would lose all contact with the outside world. No radios or newspapers were allowed in the prison. The only outside information that was allowed to penetrate the prison walls was news of the inmate's immediate family.

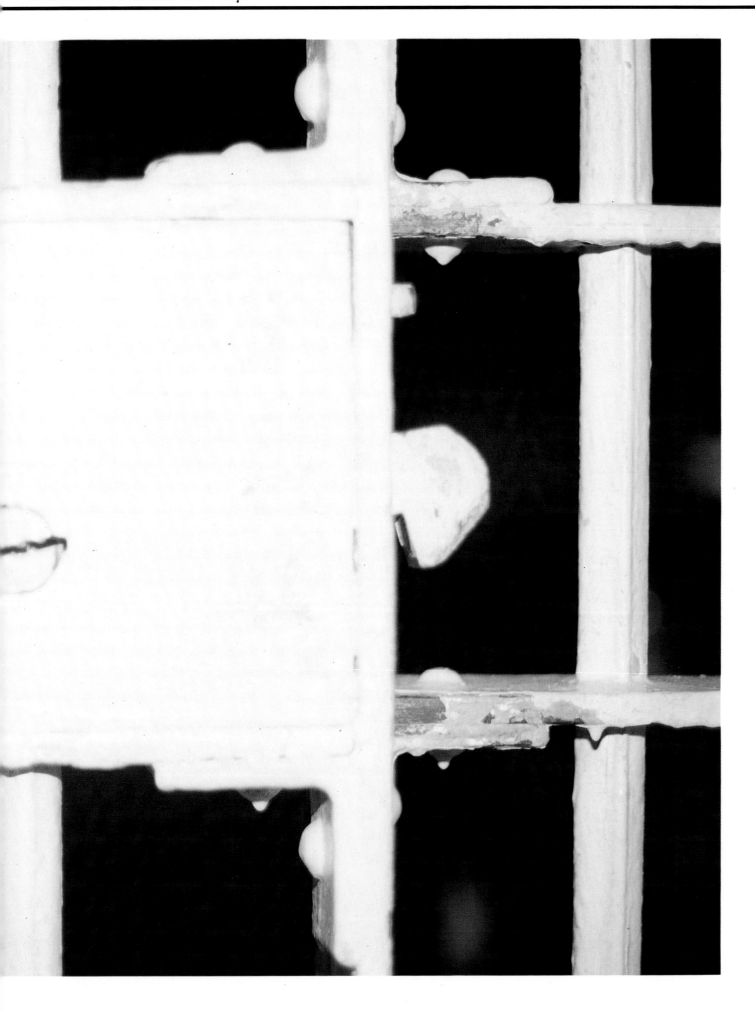

Alcatraz Island, once the most infamous prison in America. Its inmates consisted of hardened criminals, many of whom were murders. In its hey day, Alcatraz was considered to be escape proof. It was closed in 1963. Now the island and former prison is open to the public as a part of the Golden Gate National Recreation Area.

A "heartbroken" Loeb (in overcoat, extreme right) helps police search a field for his friend Bobby Frank's belt.

The second ransom note instructed Mr. Franks to take a particular south-bound train, watch for a certain factory building and throw the cigar box from the fast moving train as soon as it went past the building. He never did that. He never even went to the drugstore to retrieve the note. As soon as he hung up the phone the police called. They informed the distraught father they had found his son's body in the wetlands. So much for the "Supermen's" attempt at the perfect murder.

Leopold and Loeb were not too worried when the story exploded in the daily newspapers, after all there was still nothing to connect them to the murder—nothing but a curious reporter and a pair of horn-rimmed glasses. The eyeglasses were found near the body. Under murky circumstances a reporter for a daily newspaper gained possession of them and proceeded to find the owner. One would reasonably expect the police to undertake this task, but they were operating under two other assump-

tions; the glasses were found with other debris in the area and tracing the ransom note was a more a promising lead.

In their examination of the ransom note the officers noticed that kidnapped was spelled with one "p." There was only one conclusion to be drawn from this clue, one of Robert Franks' teachers killed the boy! They immediately arrested three of the murdered teenager's instructors.

While the teachers were being grilled under a bare light bulb, the reporter was visiting almost every optician in the Chicago area. After a week he found one who had sold Leopold a very similar pair of spectacles. The police were notified and they went to the Leopold mansion and questioned the teenager.

At first the killer did not even think they were his eyeglasses. He invited the police to search the house. Leopold was sure the police would find his pair of glasses and he would be off the hook. They didn't, but there still was not enough evidence to make him

Nathan Leopold's portable Underwood typewriter inspected by investigators. Originally the police had overlooked the typewriter on first their visit to Leopold's house. It took a persistent reporter to suspect that some typewritten essays Leopold wrote while attending the University of Chicago may have been typed on the same typewriter as the ransom note. Police later confirmed the reporter's suspicions.

a suspect. He simply told the investigators that he probably dropped the spectacles at Hegewich while bird watching. Under normal circumstances this was a reasonable enough story since Leopold was known in bird watching circles for his observations of the Kirtland Warbler.

Unknown to the teenager, the reporter had entered with the police. No one asked him for his identification and he roamed through the house with the investigators. He wasn't looking for the horn-rimmed eyeglasses, the reporter was looking for another clue, anything promising would do. He found it in the form of some typewritten essays Leopold wrote while attending the University of Chicago. Police analysis confirmed the reporter's suspicions. The

essays were typed on the same typewriter as the ransom note.

Nietzschean Supermen have an unswerving belief in their intellectual superiority. Leopold had a ready alibi for the night of the murder. He was with his respected fellow member of the community, Richard Loeb. They were both in the company of two ladies of the night who, after their private party in the back of the car, they left stranded in one of the city's parks. Unfortunately for Leopold, he had implicated his fellow murderer, someone the police would never have thought of questioning.

The police were fairly sure they would never recover the stolen typewriter, but Leopold's essays were very incriminating. Now all they needed was to

It was Darrow's long term commitment to abolition of capital punishment that gave him the idea to have his clients plead guilty and
then claim there were mitigating circumstance, thus saving his
clients from the death penalty. According to Darrow the mitigating
circumstances were the varying degrees of insanity of his clients.

Richard Leopold and Nathan Loeb after their arrest.

wrap their case up in one neat package. To this end investigators questioned the teenagers separately. Loeb broke down and confessed. When confronted with his partner's confession, Leopold acknowledged his part in the murder.

The story of two wealthy teenagers committing murder for the thrill of the experience was quite bizarre, but what made this case even more unusual was the defense counsel hired by the boy's father. He was none other than the famous Clarence Darrow!

Darrow was a defense lawyer whose work in many dramatic criminal trials earned him a place in American legal history. He was also well known as a public speaker, debater and writer. As well as his criminal work, Darrow had a national reputation as a labor lawyer. In 1902-03 he represented the miners in arbitration hearings during the Pennsylvania anthracite coal strike. Darrow's blistering cross-examination illuminated not only the horrific conditions in the mines, but also the abusive use of child labor.

The Leopold and Loeb case was to pose a particu-

larly difficult challenge for Darrow, because he was defending clients who had taken his advice and pled guilty to murder! On the face of it, the guilty plea should have ended the case in a day. Yet the case still had to be heard, but not by a hostile jury, who would have been overtly influenced by the horror of the crime and more subtilely by anti-semitism. It would be heard by a judge. Darrow's objective was to convince Chief Justice John B. Caverly that there were mitigating circumstances and save his clients from the death penalty.

Illinois State's Attorney Robert E. Crowe was shocked by the guilty plea. Under the state law he had to prove his case even though the defendants had confessed to the crime. Crowe took eight days and 80 witnesses to complete the prosecution's case. Darrow said almost nothing as the facts and testimonies flooded the courtroom. Even Leopold testified for Crowe. The spectators believed there was little for Darrow to do but wrap up his case as quickly as possible. They were wrong for the real

Richard Leopold (left) and Nathan Loeb (right) after being sentenced to life in prison. Loeb was killed by an inmate in 1936. Leopold was paroled in 1958 after after taking part as a guinea pig in anti-malaria drug experiment. He died in 1971 of a heart attack.

courtroom battle was about to begin.

On July 30 Darrow fired his first salvo; it came in the form of the thorniest of legal questions at the time. Was there such a thing as degrees of mental responsibility short of insanity in the legal sense? What!? The state's attorney returned fire immediately. How dare the defense pull a stunt like this. Crowe claimed under law it was all or nothing. "Either you are entirely responsible for your acts, or you are not responsible at all." There were no shades of grey.

Not so, argued Darrow. Since his defendants had pled guilty to the murder charge, they could not argue insanity. But proof of criminal abnormality was a mitigating circumstance, and that form of character aberration was thus a sign of diminished mental responsibility.

The debate raged for three days. Finally Judge

Caverly asserted that "the court is of the opinion that it is his duty to hear any evidence that the defense presents and it is not for the court to determine in advance what it may be."

This opened the door for what must have been to 1924 America a bizarre parade of specialists. In those days most people never heard of multiple personalities, paranoia, neurosis, the subconscious and other psychological terms. Anyone who practiced any form of psychology was usually called an "alienist," perhaps reflecting a prejudice that the study of the inner workings of the mind was somehow un-American.

Crowe shared in this common prejudice. In his summation to the court he complained, "I have heard so many big words and foreign words in this case that I sometimes thought that perhaps we were letting error creep into the record, so many foreign

Darrow (center) was a defense lawyer whose work in many dramatic criminal trials earned him a place in American legal history. When he took on the Leopold and Loeb defense he shocked the court by pleading his clients guilty.

words were being used here, and the constitution provides that these trials must be conducted in the English language."

In essence Darrow's expert witnesses said that Leopold and Loeb were products of unhealthy and restrictive childhoods. To compensate for this arrested development they became enmeshed in an abnormal fantasy life which substituted for natural emotional growth. Both Leopold and Loeb fed each other's fantasies to the point that the two teenagers never had an outside frame of reference in which to test their personal realities.

Crowe countered with his own specialists. The state's attorney managed to get each one of his experts to agree that Leopold and Loeb showed no evidence of mental disease. It was a draw. Both groups of psychiatrists had given an opposing diagnosis, setting the stage for the last battle of the trial, the summations.

It was a lopsided fight from the start. In terms of verbal and legal fireworks it may have been one of the 10 best courtroom battles of the century as Dar-

row defended "these hated, despised outcasts." He quickly ruled out the usual motives of jealousy, revenge and love. Money, which somehow was on the spectators' minds because of the ransom notes, and because it was a major part of the prosecution's case, was dismissed almost with the wave of Darrow's hand. No, the real motive was experience. The boys were obviously mentally ill, for no rational and sane man would kill just to see what it was like to commit the heinous crime.

But Darrow's real agenda was an attack on capital punishment. A fierce opponent of state sanctioned executions, Darrow had long awaited to bring his arguments in the courtroom to the defense of a client. He got to the core of the matter when he rhetorically asked the judge to consider why capital punishment still existed in a democratic society like the United States. Answering his own question with a direct reference to Leopold and Loeb, Darrow said, "You can only hang them because back of the law and back of justice and back of common instincts of man, and back of the human feeling for the young, is the

Clarence Darrow testifying for the McLeod Bill to abolish capital punishment in Washington D. C. The bill passed.

hoarse voice of the mob which says 'Kill'."

State's Attorney Crowe made the biggest blunder of his career when it came time for his summation. He could have taken almost any approach other than the one he chose and had a fighting chance. Instead, Crowe attempted to fight fire with fire. He tried to outdo Darrow's eloquence. His was such a miserable failure that toward the end of his summation he implied that if the court did not impose the death penalty the general public would believe the court had been bribed.

That the judge must have dealt with Crowe on a regular basis is almost certain. The state's attorney must have been pretty desperate to win the death penalty is also certain. He was so irrational about this case, he was willing to put his future on the line. If he did not win this point he could never appear in Judge Caverly's court again. The judge was incensed by his remark and had it stricken from the record.

Judge Caverly needed a way out of this predicament. If he found for the defense, if he indicated that

he was convinced by Darrow's argument, then he might open the door for a full scale judicial attack on capital punishment. That was the last thing Judge Caverly wanted to be known for among his peers. On the other hand, after State's Attorney Crowe's attack on his integrity there was no way he was going to find for the prosecution. He decided to sentence Leopold and Loeb to life in prison on the grounds of the defendants' ages; they were too young to be executed. As an added political measure he recommended that they not be paroled.

The trial lasted 33 days. In the end the Nietzschean Supermen were sent to Northern Illinois Penitentiary at Joliet. In 1936 Loeb was viciously slashed with a razor and killed by a fellow inmate, toward whom he had made sado-masochistic homosexual advances. Leopold concentrated on improving his already enormous intellect; he learned 37 languages and became a noted authority on several subjects. In his spare time he organized and ran the penitentiary library. In 1958 he was paroled after

Leopold and Loeb being led from the Chicago County Jail to hear their sentences.

taking part as a guinea pig in an anti-malaria drug experiment. That same year his book, *Life Plus 99 Years*, was published.

Fearing that his notoriety would follow him in the continental United States Leopold moved to Puerto Rico, where he worked as a hospital technician. In 1961 he married a doctor's widow. He died of a heart attack in 1971.

A year after the trial Clarence Darrow went on to defend John T. Scopes, a high school teacher who had broken state law by teaching the Darwinian theory of evolution in Tennessee. Although he lost, it was to be his most famous case. Darrow died in 1938 after living 80 full years.

1949
The Lonely Hearts Killers

Unlike many of today's serial killers the Lonely Hearts Murders occurred during a more trusting time. The world found out about these killings on March 2, 1949.

It was a time of great transition. World War II was over, a large part of Europe was in ruins, The Cold War had begun and The United States had just accepted responsibility for defending and maintaining the "Free World." In a few years the post-war boom would start and America would gain the highest standard of living in history.

The year before President Truman was reelected and in the process confounded pollsters by pulling the greatest upset in American history. In the same year Norman Mailer burst upon the literary scene with his novel about the war in the Pacific, *The Naked and the Dead;* General, soon to president, Dwight D. Eisenhower's *Crusade in Europe* was published; classic films such as The *Red Shoes, Bitter Rice, The Naked City* and *Oliver Twist* were shown for first time. Abstract Expressionism was about to capture the art world and for the first time shift the focus in painting from Europe to the United States. Fashion was beginning its slow exodus from Paris to New York, America was growing into a cultural colossus. The year of the growing television wave was upon us. By December 1949 about one million television sets found homes in America.

In those days people often left their doors unlocked, they didn't look over their shoulder wondering who was going to shoot them for a dollar, and the only drug 10-year-old children took was aspirin. People had neighbors in the traditional sense; neighbors who knew each other by their first names. People looked out for one another, and if they were a little nosy from time to time they meant well. Distrust, and fear of others, had yet to infuse itself into the flow of society. The Lonely Hearts killers were finally caught because Mrs. Delphine Downing's neighbors cared.

Mrs. Downing of Byron Center, a suburb of Grand Rapids, Michigan, was a 28-year-old widow.

Ever since her husband died suddenly a few years earlier, Mrs. Downing's life seemed bleak and devoid of purpose. Her only consolation was her 3-year-old daughter, Rainelle. But when Rainelle went to sleep, Delphine's long dark nights grew lonelier with each passing year. Suddenly the sun began to shine and the birds sang songs of love. A man had entered Delphine's life.

He was tall, dark and somewhat handsome, in an odd, seedy way. He was Charles Martin, a Hawaiian-born Spanish-American, who claimed to have worked for British Intelligence during the war. Martin met Mrs. Downing through a Lonely Hearts Club. His letters suggested an appealing personality who liked children. To the lonely widow and mother he sounded like a great catch.

On January 19 Martin walked into Mrs. Downing's life. He was not alone, his 28-year-old sister, "Nurse Martha," arrived with him. As Martha told the surprised Downing, "Charles on his own might have caused a bit of a scandal with the local folks. You know what it is like in these close-knit communities." Delphine was reassured by Martin's thoughtfulness and his sister's jovial manner.

The couple made their wedding plans, since the initial courtship had already been accomplished through the mail. Charles became the widow's financial adviser, which mainly meant helping her sell her property. When the sale was finalized after the wedding, they were going to move to Valley Stream, Long Island. Had Downing known the truth she would have picked up little Rainelle and run screaming from the house in fear for her life.

Charles Martin's real name was Raymond Fernandez, and Nurse Martha was really Fernandez's lover and partner in sordid crime, Martha Beck. From his teens until his early 20s Raymond was a very bashful young man. At his trial the defense,

12-02-30th.Drive,
Astoria 2, N.Y.
Dec. 14th., 48.

Dear Miss Jackson;

By virtue granted to us by the Social Club, I am taking the liberty of addressing to you this letter.

I read your description on our member lists, and liked it very much.

I am 38 years old, brown eyes, dark hair, weight 165 lbs., height 5'8". never married. Perfect health. Am considered fair looking and kind. I am living with a married sister and her husband. I am employed here with a salary of $85.00 Weekly.

If you are interested, and have not yet found a suitable correspondent, I would appreciate hearing from you, and will be more than glad to answer any questions you may wish to ask.

                          Your's Sincerely.

                                    Charles Martin

P.S.
    Enclosed, please find stamp for reply or return of letter.
                          Thank You.

Charles Martin
12-02-30th.Drive,
Astoria 2, N.Y.

Miss Alyce Jackson
304 E. 22nd.,
Fremont,
Nebraska.

In the late 40's Lonely Hearts Clubs were an acceptable means of finding a mate. Charles Martin seemed to a nice enough prospect from his letters. There were a few women who took a chance and let him into their lives. It was the last chance they would ever take, for Martin was really Raymond Fernandez, half of the Lonely Hearts Killers. Luckily for Alyse Jackson she never replied to "Mr. Martin's" letter.

Everyone thought Myrtle Young died as a result of her liver chronic ailment, although the newspapers attributed her death to cardiac failure. In truth she was killed with a massive overdose of sedatives. Fernandez later would later claim, "She croaked from over-exertion."

seeking to find extenuating circumstances, came forth with an odd explanation for his behavior. They claimed Fernandez had hit his head on a hatch while working on an oil tanker, and from that moment on the timid Raymond was transformed into a sex-crazed gigolo.

Fernandez met his 200 pound mistress the same way he met all his women—through a Lonely Hearts Club. Martha's childhood was a nightmare. She first learned about sex from one of her older brothers, who repeatedly raped her during her pre-teen years until she left home. Martha found employment as a nurse and was currently working as a matron in a home for crippled children. When she read Fernandez's initial letter she was already divorced and supporting two children of her own. Her oldest child was born out of wedlock. His father, a bus driver, committed suicide as the preferable alternative to marrying Martha.

Fernandez was living in Jane Thomson's apartment at the time he wrote to Martha. Jane Thomson was Raymond's deceased fiancée. Several months earlier she had an unfortunate accident while the couple was vacationing in Spain. The Spanish police suspected she was poisoned and had a warrant ready for Fernandez's arrest should he ever set foot in Spain again. Upon returning to New York he informed her mother that Jane died of a heart attack. After a few weeks Jane's mother vanished. Raymond told the neighbors that the poor woman was so distraught, she went to live with her son.

From her letters Martha sounded very attractive to Raymond. Unlike his usual victims who were in their 50s, Martha was 26 years old, and her maiden name was Seabrook. The appeal of her maiden name is somewhat obscure unless one knew that Fernandez practiced voodoo. William Seabrook was the author of *The Magic Island,* a virtual treasure trove of voodoo lore. According to Raymond's twisted logic, Seabrook was very magical name.

When Martha arrived at Raymond's doorstep the poor gigolo went into shock. She stood there, her face painted with cheap make up, a double chin and a head of black hair with no style; she was a mound of gross quivering flesh. Not that Fernandez was a handsome Adonis either, with his toupee and seedy Charles Boyer demeanor. But certain lonely, middle-aged women found him to be attractive. Which was more than could be said for Mrs. Beck.

They had sex the first night they met, Raymond wouldn't have it any other way, neither would Martha. Fernandez cast a cold eye at Mrs. Beck's finances, which were close to zero, and decided to drop her. Sensing that something was bothering her dream-lover, Martha turned up the sexual heat and slowly won Raymond over. She did such a good job of seducing him, using her obese body in every imaginable sexual manner, that Fernandez told Martha about his racket. "That's all right darling," she said, quite pleased with her conquest, "We can work together, I can pretend I am your sister and I can help to persuade the women to put their trust in you." Theirs was a relationship bound by some weird and bloody psychosexual/emotional glue.

For two years they preyed on lonely women, averaging about one victim a month. Most women were killed outright like the unsuspecting, 66-year-old Janet Fey of Albany, New York. Fernandez coaxed Fey to move in with him and his sister at their Valley Stream, Long Island home by promising her marriage. Once she was safely ensconced the murderous couple fleeced her for over $6,000. Martha, always the jealous type, couldn't stand Fey sharing the same bed with her Raymond, and bashed the poor woman's head in with a hammer. Janet didn't die right away, so Nurse Martha finished the senior citizen off by strangling her with a scarf.

Hurriedly, the couple wiped up Fey's blood from the floor. The poor woman had bled so much that her murderers were afraid it would leak through the floorboards and into the apartment below. When they were finished cleaning up all the bloody puddles, Raymond and Martha made passionate love next to Janet's still warm and very dead body. Mrs. Fey was packed into a trunk, and Fernandez temporarily stored the trunk his sister's house.

Several weeks later Raymond moved the trunk, reeking with the smell of Fey's dead body, to a house in South Ozone Park, Queens, New York. The couple pretended to rent the house just so they could have access to the basement. A few hours after arriving they dug up the cellar floor, buried the trunk and cemented over the hole. Four days later the cement dried, and Fernandez told the rental agent the house was unsuitable for their purposes. Once the Fey episode was over it was on to the next Lonely Hearts victim.

Myrtle Young was yet another unwary victim, but, unlike most of the women, she was killed slowly, after the wedding. She married Raymond on August 14, 1948. After the wedding the couple moved into a boarding house in Chicago, Illinois. As usual "Sister Martha" came along as part of the package. Not only did Martha move in, she slept in the same bed. When Myrtle complained about the unusual arrangement, Beck forced her to take massive doses of barbiturates.

To hasten Myrtle's demise the couple forced their latest victim to take part in round-the-clock sex with both them. Each would take turns having sex with

Jane Wilson, a home economics teacher, lived with her mother in
New York City. Fernandez took her on a vacation trip to Spain
where she died of a "heart attack." The Spanish police suspected poisoning, and had an outstanding warrant for Fernandez's arrest
should he ever return to Spain.

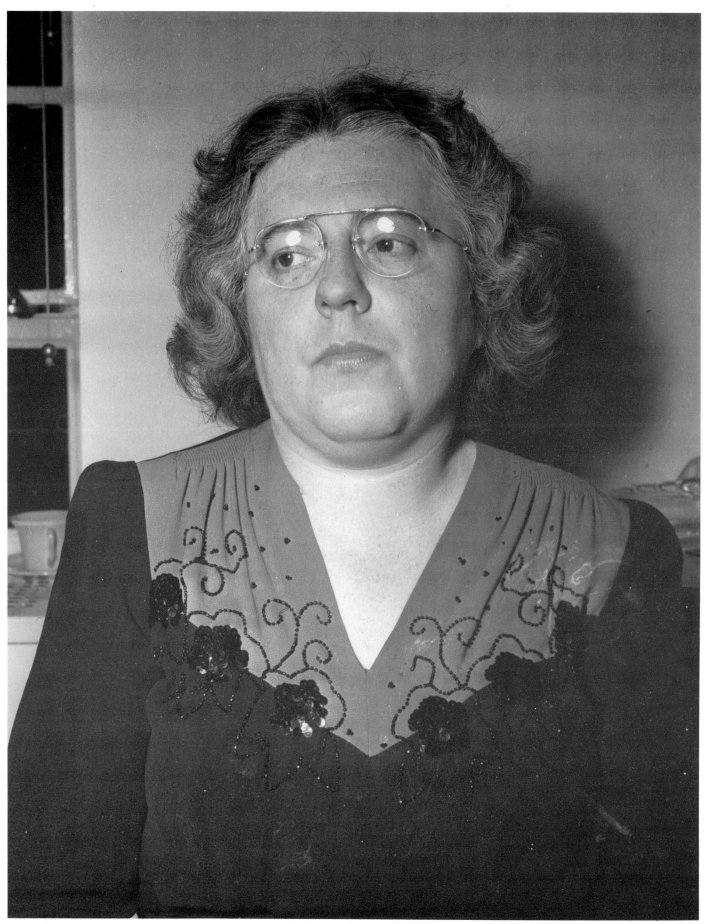

It took Esther Henne a month of marriage to figure out that all Raymond Fernandez wanted was her money. She quickly left with her savings and life intact.

Mrs. Young while the other one slept. Finally the sexual tag-team grew tired of Mrs. Young. They stuffed her with more sedatives and put her on a bus bound for her hometown in Arkansas, $4,000 poorer. The unfortunate Myrtle died in a hospital a few days later. Everyone thought it was the result of her chronic liver ailment. Fernandez would later claim, "She croaked from over-exertion."

Most of Fernandez and Beck's victims were murdered, but a few of Raymond's earlier marks were just abandoned after he had vacuumed out their bank accounts. He never divorced these women since that would entail disclosing his current location. Thus, bigamy was added to his list of crimes.

Most of the couple's murders were committed because of Martha's jealousy. According to Beck's understanding of the plan, Fernandez was not supposed to have fun; this was business. Whenever Fernandez had sex with one of the Lonely Hearts, Beck would seethe in the other room. More often than not these hateful feelings would end in an unsuspecting woman being suddenly and brutally murdered.

For two years everything seemed to go well for the bizarre duo, but good things do not last forever. It was Mrs. Downing's neighbors who brought an end to their bloody scam.

After five weeks of courtship Fernandez was just an altar trip away from getting his hands on another large sum of money. Unexpectedly, Delphine grew suspicious of Martin and his sister, and wanted to postpone the wedding for a while. Raymond was already sleeping with Mrs. Downing and Martha's jealousy had reached the point of deadly rage. Once more the barbiturates came out, and once more the little pills were poured down a victim's throat.

Delphine didn't die right away. Raymond and Martha thought this was very inconsiderate of the young woman, so one of them shot her in the head. Now Fernandez found he had a new problem to contend with. Three-year-old Rainelle was crying "Mummy, where's my Mummy," all the time.

To assuage Rainelle, the dim-witted Martha bought her a puppy. Of course the dog didn't make the tyke forget about her mother, so Beck had no other choice but to throw the child into a bathtub full of water and hold her down until she drowned. They buried both mother and child in the basement and a few days later used their standard method of dealing with dead bodies—wet cement. Afterwards Martha called Mrs. Downing's neighbors and told them Delphine had gone away for a few days and she was looking after Rainelle. With everything neatly in place the couple went to the movies.

The neighbors never took a liking to Fernandez and his sister. The flurry of phone calls explaining Downing's absence made them suspicious, so her friends made some phone calls of their own—to the police. When Fernandez and Beck came home the police were waiting for them.

One can imagine how surprised the murderous duo were to see the police. After all, the forces of law and order hadn't taken an interest in their activities before; there seemed to be no special reason why the police should be interested now. Fernandez invited the police inside. The couple were questioned about Mrs. Downing. To the most pertinent queries Raymond replied he didn't know where Delphine was or when she would return. As an evasive fog settled about the couple, the police turned their attentions to the house. Sensing the shift of attention and to forestall any more embarrassing questions, Fernandez confidently told the police, "Go ahead, search the house if you want to."

The investigators began their search by casually poking about Mrs. Downing's home. They would open a drawer here and pick up a pillow there. Small indications that something was amiss kept showing up, for instance, Rainelle's toys were still laying around the house and Mrs. Downing's letters were on the table, opened. Simultaneously the investigators had the same idea—let's look in the basement. On the way downstairs the policemen all noticed a wet patch in the cement floor. To the trained eye it was almost as if the site had a neon sign that said, "look at this." It had a peculiar grave-like shape. The investigators needed no prompting to dig up the damp spot. After arduously digging down 4 feet they found two bodies. Rainelle's body was lying on top of her mother's.

Much is made today about the circumstances surrounding a criminal's confession. In the case of Fernandez and Beck there was no ambiguity; they began confessing to various murders almost as soon as they got to the station house. The Grand Rapids police rightly felt they had two of the vilest murderers they had ever come across. Since Michigan did not have a death penalty, the maximum sentence the pair could receive was life in prison. There was also the possibility that the couple might be paroled in 15 years. The investigators thought this was a travesty of justice. But, unwittingly, Martha and Raymond did themselves in; they confessed to Janet Fey's murder. Janet Fey was killed and buried in New York, and that state did have a death penalty.

The first indication Fernandez and Beck had that they talked too freely about their exploits came when Michigan's attorney general ordered a postponement of their trial. He was giving New York state a chance to extradite the couple free of judicial complications. Once Martha and Raymond realized

Raymond Fernandez and Martha Beck's last victims were Mrs. Delphine Downing and her 21-month-old daughter Rainelle of Grand Rapids, Michigan. Their bodies were found by the police packed in cement in the basement of Mrs. Downing's house.

Grand Rapids, Michigan detectives look for more evidence in Mrs. Downing's clothing trunks. Mrs. Downing's neighbors alerted police to mother and daughter's strange disappearance and the odd behavior of Downing's new husband and sister-in-law, Raymond Fernandez and Martha Beck.

After removal of Janet Fey's body from the South Ozone Park basement Nassau County Police seized a trunk belonging to Fernandez's
sister. At the time investigators thought that this trunk was used to
transport Fey's body to the basement.

The New York police removing Janet Fey's body from the South Ozone Park house. When the murderous couple confessed, they included among their victims Janet Fey. They buried her body in a basement at South Ozone Park, Queens, New York. It was this murder that sent them to the electric chair.

Martha Beck enjoyed her last moments in the sunshine. On August 22, 1949 a prison guard escorted Beck to the entrance of Sing Sing Prison where she would soon be executed for the Lonely Hearts murders.

Raymond Fernandez after his arrest for the murder of Mrs. Delphine Downing and her 21-month-old daughter Rainelle.

what was happening their lawyers fought back and lost. Thirty days later the Lonely Hearts killers were behind bars in Long Island.

To pass the time before and during the trial the couple read paperback murder novels. The newspapers thought this was a significant fact and kept track of what novels each of the murderers read. Once the trial began reporters had other and more interesting events to report. The couple pleaded not guilty by reason of insanity. Martha's history of childhood sexual abuse became part of her defense. All aspects of Fernandez and Beck's lurid sexual lives were brought out during the trial. At one point the jury was given a visual demonstration of the lustful nature of the couple's relationship.

Martha, dressed in a shapeless silk dress and wearing a thick cake of rouge and a heavy smear of cheap, red lipstick, was being led to the witness stand to testify in her own behalf. As she was walking past Raymond an outrageous impulse took control of her and she suddenly broke free of the two courtroom guards. Martha wrapped herself around Fernandez and kissed him on the face, neck and mouth. At the same time Beck was furiously bumping and grinding her obese body against her former lover. It took several guards to pull Martha off of Raymond. When the couple was finally pulled apart, Beck screamed to the jury, "I love him! I do love him, and I always will."

In spite of all their theatrics, the couple was found guilty of first degree murder. A few days later the judge sentenced them to death by electrocution in Sing Sing Prison's electric chair. Although the executions were set for August 22, 1949, due to various legal appeals the death penalty wasn't carried out until March 8,1951.

Fate can play strange tricks on people. When Raymond and Martha arrived in Sing Sing, they were placed in cells that allowed them to see each other through an open door that separated the men's and women's wings of Death Row. Seeing each other, waving and blowing kisses to each other, strengthened their emotional bonds. His daily sighting of Beck encouraged Fernandez to brag about his sexual exploits. The prison psychiatrist believed Raymond's boasting was a way of showing he was not afraid of facing death. His fellow prisoners were quickly fed up with listening to his stories and called him the "Mail Order Romeo."

During the 18 months the couple awaited the disposition of their appeals they wrote letters to each other on a weekly basis. Most of the time Martha promised her love would remain true beyond the electric chair. For one brief moment the couple had a lover's quarrel. Beck discovered that Fernandez

Martha Beck questioned by Grand Rapids, Michigan detectives for the murder of Mrs. Downing and her daughter.

was telling the male prisoners about her odd fetishes. She exploded in her next letter, "You are a double crossing, two timing skunk. I learn now that you have been doing quite a bit of talking to everyone. It's nice to learn what a terrible, murderous person I am, while you are such a misunderstood, white-haired boy, caught in the clutches of a female vampire."

Before their executions the couple made up. Just prior to his, Raymond wrote a last note to Martha, "People want to know whether I still love Martha. But of course I do. I want to shout it out. I love Martha. What does the public know about love?"

At Sing Sing, when there was more than one execution scheduled for the same day, the weaker prisoner went first. On March 8 four executions were planned. Two men convicted for murder and armed robbery went first. They were led weeping and shaking all the way into the "little green room." The big question among the prison population was which of the Lonely Hearts killers would die last.

Martha was deemed to be the stronger of the two. Raymond's bravado broke on the way to his execution. His legs sagged and he had to be propped up for the last few feet into the room. Martha went next, and it is said that she sat in the electric chair with a "Mona Lisa-like" smile on her face.

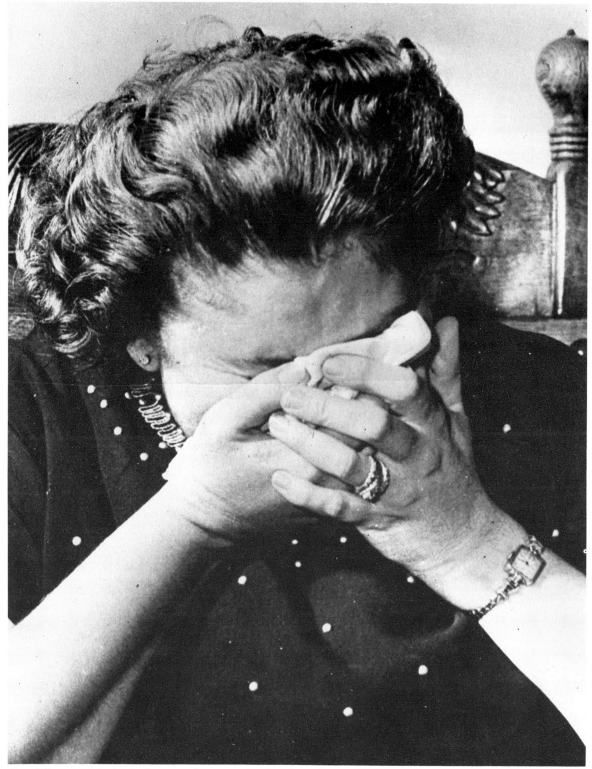

Even killers cry. Martha Beck weeps after giving the Grand Rapids police the gory details of her and Raymond Fernandez's killing spree.

Before she took her last walk, Martha Beck spoke a few parting words: "My story is a love story, but only those tortured with love can understand what I mean. I was pictured as a fat, unfeeling woman. True I am fat, but, if that is a crime, how many of my sex are guilty?"

"I am not unfeeling, stupid or moronic. I am a woman who had a great love and will always have it.

Imprisonment in the 'Death House' has only strengthened my feeling for Raymond. My last words and my last thoughts will be: Let him who is without sin cast the first stone."

One wonders how Martha and Raymond's brutally murdered victims would have viewed such mawkish sentiments.

1963
Terror Comes to Boston

The youngest president of the United States, John F. Kennedy, was in office in 1963, and the Camelot of the Sixties was in full swing. In those years the center of the political, social, military and cultural universe seemed to reside in Washington, D.C. and the president's home state, Massachusetts, was the proudest in the nation.

That year saw a breeze of change begin to blow in America; by the end of decade it would become a gale force storm. In those sunny days of incredible American wealth and power a new generation was finding its voice. Singers such as Joan Baez and Bobby Dylan were leading the chorus. The rock and roll hit *Those Hazy, Crazy Days of Summer*, seemed to sum up a year of promise.

However, Boston, Massachusetts was in the grip of an icy reign of terror. A faceless killer was stalking the streets. His victims were young and old women and his murders were especially brutal. He terrorized a wide area including Boston, Lynn, Cambridge and Salem, yet he became known and famous as the Boston Strangler.

In 1931 Albert DeSalvo was born to a troubled family. His father, a plumber by trade, regularly beat his mother in front of Albert and his two sisters. Sometimes his father used to beat the whole family. DeSalvo's earliest memories of these beatings occurred when he was 3 or 4 years old. Albert watched in horror as his father broke his mother's hand during an alcoholic fit of abuse. As his mother began to wail in pain, he and his sisters ran through the house crying. The elder DeSalvo followed and beat them until the police came and put a stop to the family violence. Occasionally Albert's father would bring a prostitute home and slap his wife around in front of the whore for his own amusement.

To escape the relentless beatings at home Albert would take off for Noodle Island, in East Boston, with his sisters and hide under the piers, wharfs and in the warehouses during the day. They were not alone. The area, at night, was crawling with children like themselves, some younger, some older, all dangerous. Like a pack of rats that fall upon one of their own who is lame or infirm, the children would attack drunks in numbers often as high as 30. Their victims never had a chance and usually ended up being fished out of the harbor the next day, torn apart and very dead. Those who lived near Noodle Island called the children "wharf rats." If you knew about the wharf rats, you knew enough to stay away from the piers when the sun went down. Albert's father had a fair idea what would happen to him if went to look for his children when they ran away. The elder DeSalvo never went to Noodle Island.

DeSalvo was a very shy child and didn't like to fight; he never took part in the wharf rats' attacks. There was never the pressing need of sheer survival for Albert and his sisters. As bad as it might be, they had a home. There was barely enough food for the DeSalvo family. Although they never starved or went hungry, they were not able to push themselves away from the table with a full stomach. This unfulfilled feeling was to remain with Albert for the rest of his life.

If there was a sexual Olympic event Albert would have held the gold medal for decades. But sexual gratification eluded DeSalvo. He had the capacity to have an endless series of orgasms every five minutes. This led to an odd sort of popularity in his neighborhood. In his teenage years he was bisexual. Most of the men he had sex with paid for it and this was fine with Albert since he always needed money. Even though he gained momentary release from his homosexual encounters, he preferred women.

In fact DeSalvo desired women, regardless of age or looks. "...but it really was Woman that I wanted - not any special one, just Woman with what a woman has. I didn't even care so much what she looked like, or how old she was, it was Woman that I wanted."

Another factor became enmeshed in DeSalvo's chaotic personality, that of burglary, or as Albert called it B & E, short for the police classification of breaking and entering. He started stealing at age five, with his father teaching him the ropes. By the time he was 12 he graduated from petty theft to breaking and entering. After his second arrest DeSalvo was sent to the Lyman School for Delinquent Boys.

Like many other correctional institutions the lessons learned at the Lyman School were not the

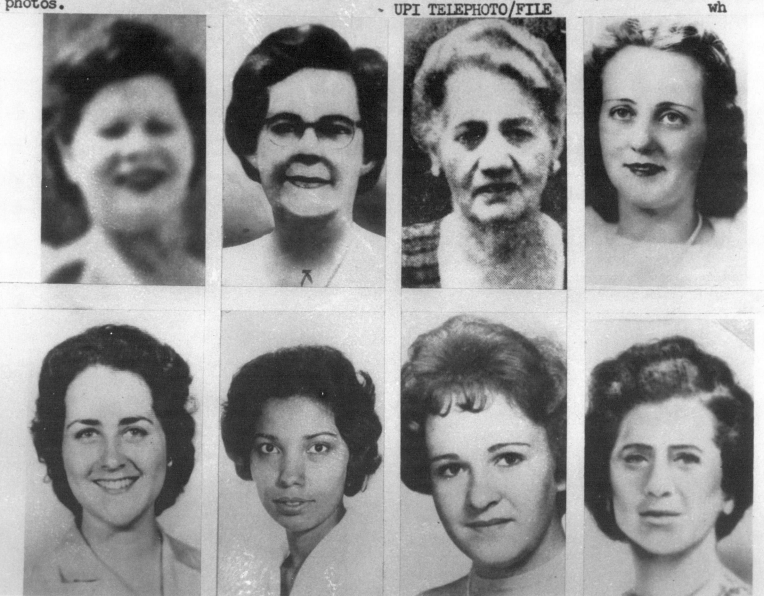

SPECIAL FOR CAPE COD STANDARD TIMES
NXP1407819-FILE-1/6/64-NEW YORK: Upper left to lower right are: Rachel Lazarus,Helen E.
Ida Irga,Mrs. J. Delaney,Patricia Bissette,Daniela M. Saunders,Mary A. Sullivan,Mrs. Isra
Goldberg. All of whom have been strangled in the Boston area recently.are shown in file
photos.
                                          - UPI TELEPHOTO/FILE   wh

*Eight of the Boston Strangler's victims. From upper left to lower
right: Rachel Lazarus, Helen E. Blake, Ida Irga, Mrs. J. Delaney,
Patricia Bissette, Daniela M. Saunders, Mary A Sullivan, Mrs. Israel
Goldberg.*

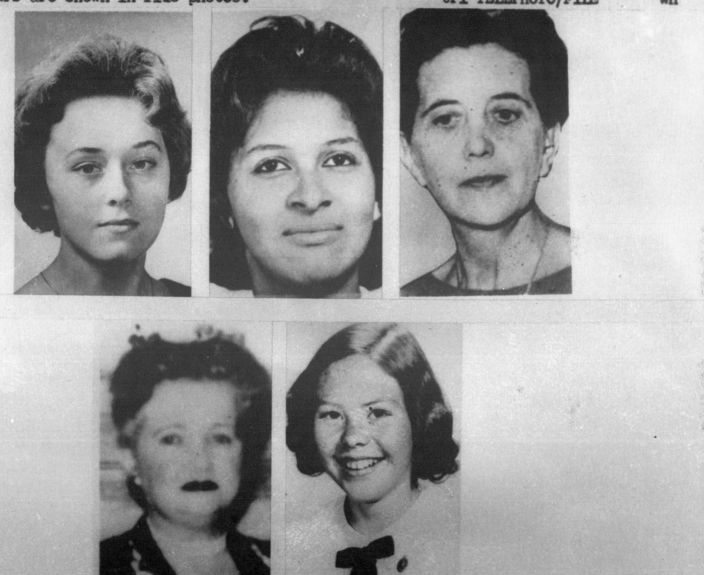

Six of the Boston Strangler's thirteen victims. From upper left to lower right: Margaret Cadigan, Sophie Clark, Anna E. Slessers, Jane Sullivan, Cheryl Laird.

subjects that were formally taught. Albert said it best in his own crude way, "Lyman School is supposed to be a place where bad boys are taught to be good. That's a laugh, ain't it? . . . .When you get out of Lyman School you know how a criminal thinks and you are a boy who knows a lot about sexual perversion."

In his late teens DeSalvo joined the army and became, by all outward appearances, a model soldier. His attention to the rules, to his officers, to maintaining the best spit-and-polish image earned him the honor of Colonel's Orderly 27 times. It was while stationed in Germany that DeSalvo, the shy little abused child, became the U.S. Army's European Middleweight Boxing Champion for two straight years. DeSalvo the soldier pursued his compulsions too, in his spare time he seduced quite a few absent officers' wives. There were even rumors of orgies that would go on till dawn, and some law enforcement officials suspected that he committed several rapes during his army enlistment.

As unlikely as it might seem, DeSalvo found time to marry his wife Irmgard, a proper, middle-class German woman. Albert would later say she was cold, proper and sexually repressed. A very strange match indeed for a man with such appetites. Albert DeSalvo left the army to return to Boston with his wife and work as a handyman and a burglar.

On June 14, 1962, the killer stalked the corridors of a Back Bay, Boston apartment house. He had picked the building at random and wandered the halls. He read the names that were alongside the doors. The killer was looking for a woman's name, not a particular woman, just any woman.

Mrs. Anna Slesers was a 55-year-old Latvian immigrant who had been divorced for 20 years. She lived alone and had a 25-year-old son, Juris. She heard a knock on her door and responded. A voice told her that the landlord had sent him, "to do some work in your apartment." Anna let the man in.

The killer knew that apartment house dwellers always needed something fixed, they responded positively to having their quarters repaired. The man followed Slesers into her bathroom where she pointed out some task to be done. Anna received a blow to the head with a heavy blunt object for her troubles. Blood gushed from her head like an uncapped oil well. She may have still been alive when the intruder put a belt around her neck and sexually assaulted her, but moments later she was dead.

Robbery was not his motive, but he rummaged around the apartment looking through Slesers' drawers and closets. It was a mindless act, like a zombie going through the motions of a robbery. He looked at everything, but stole nothing. The attacker

washed Anna's blood off his and face, and to hide his blood-soaked clothes the killer wore Juris' raincoat which he found hanging in the closet.

Juris Slesers arrived at his mother's apartment shortly before 8 p.m. and knocked on the door. He was anxious to be on time to drive Anna to a service at a nearby Latvian church. Not only were these services spiritually comforting to his mother, but they provided a connection to the homeland she was forced to flee after the Soviet occupation.

He knocked again; there was no answer. Not a sound could be heard inside the apartment. A wet wave of fear rose from Juris' stomach and he fought it back by loudly banging his fists on the door. A chilling silence answered him. Anxiety and dread took control of Juris. He took a few steps back and flung himself at the door. With a splintering crack the door burst open.

Inside the apartment Juris was greeted with silence and darkness. He walked into a misplaced chair in the narrow hallway. Even before Anna's son turned on the lights he knew his mother's orderly home had been violated. He fearfully searched the ransacked apartment for his mother. Juris found her lying on her back, her legs spread wide apart, in a short hallway between the kitchen and bathroom. The blue housecoat she always wore was flung open, revealing her nakedness. Around her neck was the blue sash belonging to the housecoat. It was tied in the form of crude grotesque little girl's bow.

The police arrived at the crime scene and due to a lack of clues concluded that a burglar had entered the apartment and surprised a scantily clad Mrs. Slesers. Overcome by sexual desire, the theory continued, the intruder assaulted Anna. When the burglar was finished he became fearful Slesers would call the police so he strangled her. It all seemed quite reasonable to the police; it was an isolated bungled robbery attempt which resulted in murder. They had no way of knowing this was the beginning of the Boston Strangler's reign of terror.

In fact it took a while for the police to realize they had a serial killer on their hands. Two weeks later the Strangler killed 85-year-old Mary Mullen. Again using the maintenance man ruse he gained entrance to her apartment. As soon as her back was turned he put his arm around her neck and squeezed. This was to become one of his standard methods of attack. Mary was literally scared to death. She went limp and died in the Strangler's arms. He laid her on the sofa and left without leaving his usual trademarks of sexual assault, the ransacked apartment and the little girl's bow tied somewhere on the body. The police assumed Mullen had died of natural causes. It was only after an au-

Nineteen year old Mary A. Sullivan's murder catapulted the Boston Strangler case to the front pages of the Boston newspapers again. The news media gathered in front of her apartment house like vultures. They stayed long into the night waiting for juicy tidbits of information.

The Boston police desperately search for clues on the roof adjoining Mary A. Sullivan's apartment. Ms. Sullivan was the Boston Strangler's 13th and last victim. But law enforcement officials in the Boston area couldn't have known that at the time.

Albert DeSalvo, the Boston Strangler, shown here captured after his failed escape from Bridgewater State Hospital.

topsy was performed that the police suspected foul play, and even then they weren't sure.

Days later, on June 30, 65-year-old retired nurse Helen Blake was murdered. Helen had been expecting a repairman after complaining about minor damage to the bedroom windows. She welcomed her murderer by commenting, "Well, it's about time."

Helen's neighbors called the police. They were worried when they did not see or hear from her for two days. She was discovered face down on her bed, naked except for the pajama tops shoved up over her shoulders. Tied around Helen's neck was her brassiere and silk stocking in the form of a bow. Needless to say her apartment had been ransacked, but nothing was stolen. Before Helen's body was turned over the police noticed that besides raping the poor woman the attacker had also bitten her in several places.

For the next few hours, after he killed Blake, the Strangler rode around the greater Boston area in a

daze, and then for no reason at all he drove into an apartment complex parking lot. Nina Nichols, a 68-year-old widow, had just returned to her apartment after a weekend visit with some friends. She called her sister, Marguerite Steadman, and made dinner arrangements for 6 p.m. Nina was in the middle of promising to be on time when her doorbell rang. The last words her sister heard from Nina were "I'll call you right back."

From the very beginning she was suspicious of the stranger claiming to be a maintenance man. In no uncertain terms she stated she might call the building supervisor. The killer was thrown off guard. He countered her threat by telling her to go ahead and call; it would be a long time before he came back to fix anything in her apartment. Against her better judgment she believed him, and the two of them walked from room to room as she pointed out the things that needed to be repaired.

Feeling he would rather not kill this woman, the

Defense attorney, F. Lee Bailey looks at a photo of his infamous
client, Albert DeSalvo, the self confessed Boston Strangler. Bailey
first gained international notoriety for his success in gaining an ac-
quittal in the Dr. Sam Sheppard murder trail.

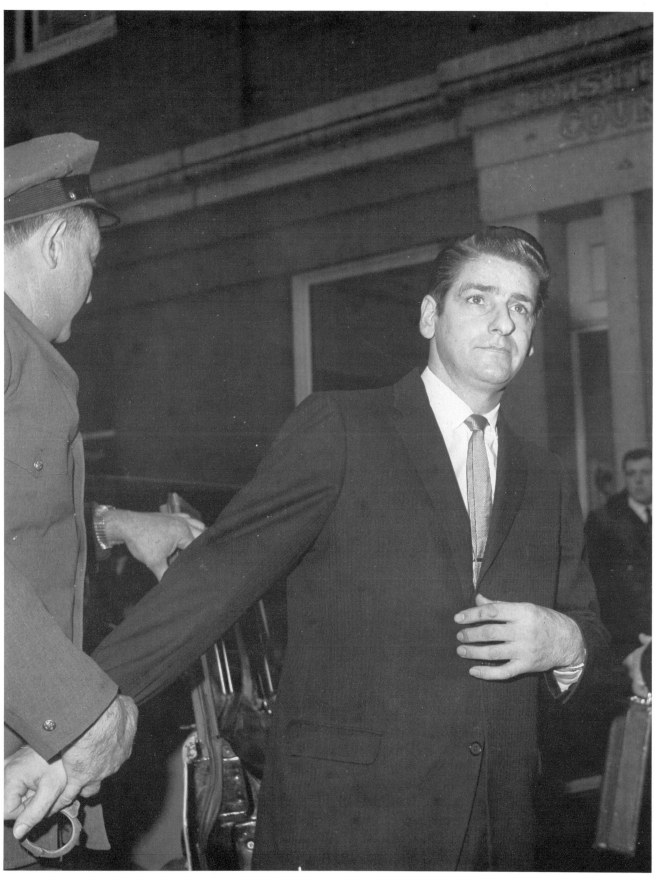

The Boston Strangler was never caught by the police, Albert DeSalvo
confessed to the brutal murders while awaiting trail on sexual assault and burglary charges. What made his confession believable
was the wealth of unpublished details he provided, then, Assistant
Attorney General John S. Bottomley.

Strangler followed Nina, pretending to make mental notes of the work to be done. But before they reached the bedroom Nichols turn her back on the killer. An impulse, like a growing electrical charge, changed the Strangler's mind and he grabbed Nina's neck from behind. They tumbled backwards onto the bed. A brief struggle ensued; the killer tried to strangle Nina with a belt, but it broke. He urgently groped around for something else and found one of the victim's nylon stockings. Quickly the killer wrapped it around her neck before she could scream. It didn't break. Nina died.

By 7:30 p.m. the Steadmans were worried. Nina Nichols was never this late. Mr. Steadman called the building's janitor. He confirmed that Nina's car was still parked on the street and agreed to go to Nichols' apartment to investigate.

The janitor knocked on the door, waited about a minute, knocked again, and then let himself in with a pass key. He must have had an uneasy feeling about what he might find before he entered. As he suspected, the place had been ransacked. What he was not prepared for was finding Nina Nichols on her back with a bow made of nylon stockings tied around her neck, and a wine bottle rammed into her private parts. And so it went victim after victim, and the elderly women of Boston went into a state of fear and panic.

Initially police jurisdictions were split. Soon there would be five departments involved: Cambridge, Lawrence, Lynn, Salem and Boston. Law enforcement officials were groping in the dark for suspects. At first prostitutes were asked about their odd clients whose tastes bordered on the violent and kinky. When this did not pan out investigators picked up and questioned peeping-toms, elevator feelers, obscene phone callers and anybody else who committed sexual misdemeanors. All these efforts led to naught, and the murders went on.

On August 19, 1962 a 75-year-old widow, Ida Irga, living in a fashionable section of Boston was the Strangler's fifth victim. She was found lying on her back with her legs propped up on two chairs and spread apart, grotesquely mimicking the gynecological examination position. She had been sexually assaulted and her apartment had been ransacked.

Victim number six, a 67-year-old nurse, Jane Sullivan, was killed the next day, but the police didn't find her body until 10 days later. When they did discover the corpse, it was badly decomposed due to the hot August heat.

Massachusetts Attorney General Edward M. Brooke knew something had to be done to break the stalled investigations. He appointed Assistant Attorney General John S. Bottomley to head a coordinated

Strangler Bureau. All the involved police departments had to work with the task force and pool their information.

It took a while for the Strangler Bureau to sift through and coordinate all the files they were given. In the meantime the killer had temporarily ceased his crimes, giving investigators a reprieve to ponder his next move. Since three out of six of the Strangler's victims were health care professionals, some of the investigators thought this was an important clue. Like many other theories about the killer, this too fizzled out.

Thanksgiving came and went and there were no new murders. Everything was in a state of possibilities. Perhaps the Strangler had quit for the holidays, perhaps he had left the Boston area, perhaps he died in an auto accident, perhaps, perhaps. But even though the Strangler Bureau had no new leads, they felt that if he was still alive they would catch him. The one thing the investigators did not count on was the killer abruptly changing his pattern.

On December 5 the killer was stalking an apartment house hallway again. He rang a doorbell with a woman's name on it. The voice from behind the door told the impatient murderer that her husband was in the shower and he would come and speak with the "maintenance man" as soon as he put his robe on. Shocked that he could have been so mistaken the Strangler hurried to another part of the apartment complex. He wasn't wrong, he had been deceived. There was no one else in the apartment with the frightened woman, she was just a little cautious and very lucky.

The stalker's search soon yielded three female names on a doorbell. Usually he would pass a dwelling like this up, but this time he knocked. A young, attractive black woman opened the door.

Sophie Clark, a 20-year-old Carnegie Institute student, greeted the repairman. She thought he was there to repair the faucets in the bathroom. Yet as soon as he began looking at the faucets he told Miss Clark that he took this part-time job when his modeling business was slow. He talked so fast that visions of a more glamorous life danced in the young woman's head. Sophie knew many men considered her beautiful, and this husky man's offer to set her up earning $30 to $40 a day really appealed to her. Naturally, when she was asked to turn around so he could see how she was built, she complied.

It was as if he was entering a dream-like state. When this beautiful woman turned her back toward the killer, he seemed to float over to her and his arm flowed around her neck. The trance was broken as Sophie began to struggle. Both killer and victim fell back on the sofa. She kept struggling until she lost consciousness. After the Strangler raped the bound Sophie she regained consciousness, and he had to choke her to death with three stockings to stop her .

On New Year's Eve the Strangler visited a 23-year-old Boston secretary, Patricia Bissette. He let himself into her apartment by forcing the lock with a stiff piece of plastic, resembling a thin, elongated credit card. She was standing in the living room wearing a blanket as she watched the killer enter her apartment. Incredulous at first, Patricia believed his story that he lived upstairs and was looking for her roommate. They sat down, drank coffee together and listened to Christmas carols. He would always remember this victim. "She talked to me like a man, treated me like a man."

Bissette's two roommates found her body on New Year's Day. She was tucked into bed with a sheet pulled to her neck. The horrible truth was revealed as the police removed the sheet and found her strangled with one of her own stockings, and tied in the now characteristic bow. The apartment had been ransacked and an autopsy revealed Patricia had been sexually assaulted.

The Strangler Bureau desperately moved into high gear. They employed the services of a noted psychic, Peter Hurkos. He was able to pass all of their tests as well as explain the unexpected lateness of one of the detectives, due to an unscheduled and unauthorized stop at his girl friend's house for an hour of fun. Yet when it came to locating the killer, Hurkos found a poor masochistic soul in need of psychiatric treatment instead.

Another, more traditional consultant was Dr. James A. Brussel. His claim to fame was the successful profile of New York City's "Mad Bomber." This gentle, urban terrorist plagued the city, from 1940-56, with homemade bomb explosions and letters to the daily newspapers after each attack. No one was ever killed or hurt in these explosions, but the New York Police Department believed it was only a matter of time before someone was injured.

Brussel correctly profiled the bomber as a lonely, foreign born, conservative, quiet, middle-aged man, who, when found, would be wearing a double breasted suit with all the jacket buttons fastened. His portrait became a legendary accomplishment in the annals of psychiatric profiles. Indeed, the moment George Metesky was arrested the detectives discovered that he fit the description to a tee, right down to the double breasted suit, buttoned up all the way.

But when it came to the Boston Strangler, Brussel, as well as the other members of the profile team, were completely off base. What threw the investigators off was the sudden shift in the age groups of the Strangler's victims. They conjectured that they were looking for not one but two killers.

The first killer that was profiled murdered only elderly women. The committee speculated that he was motivated by his inability to express his hostility against his domineering, punishing, yet seductive mother. It was further thought that the Strangler was impotent and lived alone, thus he had plenty of time to dwell upon the hatred and sexual desire for his mother. The blinding rage and sexual inadequacy that the killer felt were expressed by his attacks on "old women."

The profile of the second killer was vague. The committee believed the young women were possibly killed by someone who knew them, and who suppressed his homosexual tendencies. It was mistakenly thought that once the common thread of young women's murders was discovered, the police would have enough evidence to arrest him.

Investigators were no closer to the killer after eight murders as they were after the first one, and the lone Strangler was ready to kill again. With victim number nine he was back to his old habits. The killing of 69-year-old Mary Brown was brutal. Instead of strangling his victim first with his arm and waiting for her to pass out, the killer bashed her in the head with a lead pipe. Afterwards the Strangler repeatedly stabbed the woman's body with a fork until she was covered in blood. Like all his other victims, Mary Brown was strangled with a bow around her neck and sexually assaulted.

November 23, the day after President Kennedy's assassination, the Strangler wondered if killing another victim was appropriate during the period of national mourning. His murderous urges won out over common decency and 23-year-old Joann Graff was strangled. This was his 12th victim and a particularly disturbing one for the killer.

"It was a very cheap apartment, really cheap furniture, even the Salvation Army wouldn't take it. It was just like she was living out of a suitcase." Even though the shabbiness of Joann's dwelling got on the Strangler's nerves, it did not prevent him from killing again.

The next killing was to be the Strangler's last, not because he was caught, but because whatever was short-circuited in his psyche untangled itself. It also was his most brutal murder. The Strangler had raped 19-year-old Mary Sullivan while she was alive and bound her with articles of her own clothing, then he strangled her with her own leotards, then he had several orgasms on the dead body and finally he mutilated her with a broom stick. Before he left Mary's apartment he left another large bow tied under her chin and a greeting card by her left foot. The card read "HAPPY NEW YEAR."

MURDER

IN NORTH AMERICA
PORTFOLIO II

Life inside Alcatraz was far from pleasant, but contrary to Hollywood depictions and popular belief, physical mistreatment of prisons was never allowed. In fact the food inside Alcatraz was considered to be the best in the Federal prison system. Some Alcatraz's famous inmates have included: Al Capone, Alvin Karpis, George "Machine Gun" Kelly and Mickey Cohen. Perhaps the prisoner who gained the most fame while serving time inside the prison was Robert Stroud, "the Bird Man of Alcatraz." He spent his time learning about bird diseases and wrote highly respected scientific books on the subject. Often some prisoners would spend their nights thinking of ways of escaping the Island before dropping off to sleep. In its 29 years as a Federal prison, 26 inmates attempted to flee their incarceration. The score stands as 8 shot dead or drowned, 13 captured, and 5 unaccounted for. Federal authorities refuse to admit that any of the 5 were successful with their escapes.

Shortly after George Abbott assumed the identity of Frank Almy, he made his way to Hanover, a small town in western New Hampshire. Most people know of the town because Dartmouth University was, and still is located there.

In the nineteenth century the Vale of Tempe was wood glen with a small sparkling brook rushing through it. Long before Abbott killed Christine Warden in the Vale, Daniel Webster used to practice his oratory skills there with the trees standing as a mute audience. Today it is forgotten, located at the bottom of a ski run.

The most exciting event the town of Hanover had seen was an occasional fire or a small burglary. People slept comfortably in their beds until George Abbott came to town.

The residents of Hanover learned of Christine's heinous murder shortly before midnight when the great bell in Dartmouth Hall tolled.

There is no record of what the Warden barn looked like. This converted barn gives some indication of one of the styles in the area.

La Hacienda de Don Antonio Serrino Martinez in Taos, New Mexico reflects the how Antonio Chavéz and his bothers lived in the 1830's. This is a photo of the rear courtyard or "placita" with an adobe wall separating the back rooms and lean-to built of poles for the pack animals.

The Boston Strangler covered some of victims so that whoever discovered them would have a ghastly surprise.

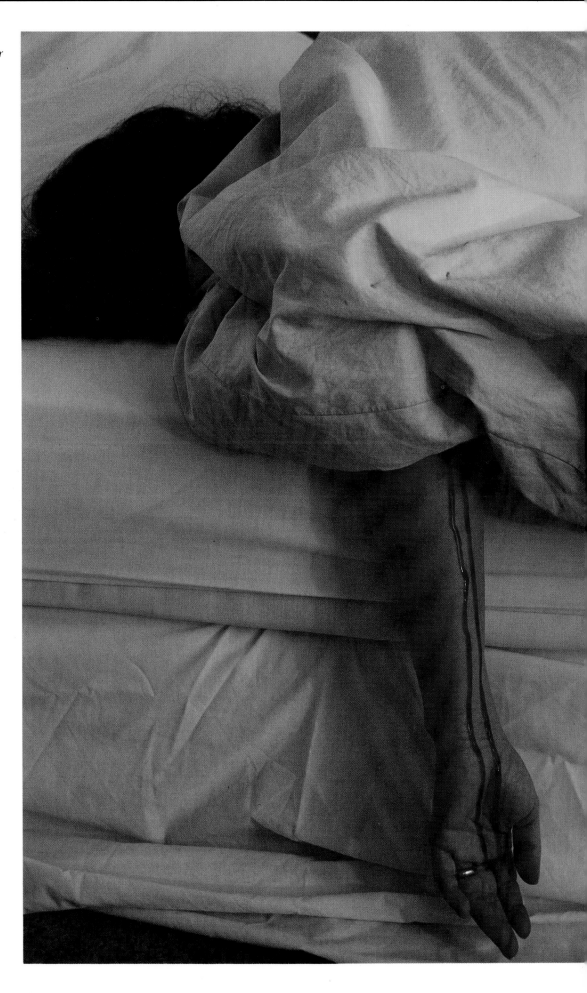

Albert DeSalvo was never convicted for the 13 Boston Strangler murders. He was sentenced to life imprisonment for 10 counts of un-related sexual assault and burglary.

After the 13th murder the Strangler only bound and raped his victims. Once, while driving around Cambridge the killer felt himself being overwhelmed by his murderous compulsive desires. He actually rang three different doorbells. When a woman answered the door to his standard maintenance man ploy, he left mumbling it was the wrong apartment. At the last apartment he broke into tears telling the occupant, "I'm sorry I don't know why I'm here."

Now more than ever the Strangler Bureau and Assistant Attorney General John S. Bottomley felt the need to apprehend this fiend. The 13th homicide was especially brutal and those investigators who saw the body were truly repulsed by the Strangler's depths of depravity. Yet there were no new leads. It was like trying to catch smoke with a net.

Albert DeSalvo could not keep out of trouble. Along with his usual breaking and entering crimes, he concocted a sexual scam for his own amusement. Long before the Boston Strangler killings, DeSalvo would ring the doorbells of single young women claiming to be a talent scout for a modeling agency. He gained entrance to their apartments by lavishly complimenting their good looks and figures. Once inside he would mention that they could earn a lucrative living as a model. Most of the women were flattered and let him record their physical statistics with a tape measure. The way Albert measured the women usually entailed a lot of fondling of legs, hips and breasts. Oddly enough most of the women complained only when it turned out that no intimate contact was forthcoming.

DeSalvo was arrested during an aborted burglary. At the station house one detective thought Albert's description matched the "Measuring Man" sex maniac, so he called in one of his victims. The woman made a positive identification and Albert was sentenced to jail for two years for burglary and assault and battery. At the time some of the police thought he was a harmless pervert. In April 1962 DeSalvo was paroled after serving 11 months, just two months before the first Boston Strangler murders.

While the police were looking for the Strangler another series of attacks were plaguing the Greater Boston Area. The perpetrator was known as the "Green Man." The Green Man was a sexual assailant and occasional rapist who wore green maintenance-man trousers and sometimes a matching green jacket. He entered his victim's dwellings by either breaking in or forcing his way through the door. Once the attacker was inside the women were made to strip at knife point, occasionally tied up, and kissed all over their bodies. His assaults infrequently ended in rape.

On October 27, 1964, the Green Man's career came to an end. At 9:30 a.m. a young Cambridge housewife was dozing in bed after seeing her husband off to work, when there was a knock at the door. Upon answering the knock the housewife saw a stocky man dressed in green trousers with his eyes hidden by large, dark green sunglasses. Claiming to be a detective he forced the woman into her bedroom. By now the housewife knew he was not from the police and demanded he leave the room at once. The assailant answered her demand by tying her to the bed. At knife point he kissed and fondled her body. After he was finished he loosened her bonds. Upon leaving he ordered her to be quiet for 10 minutes and then a strange look crossed his face. He said, "I'm sorry."

No sooner was the attacker out the door than the housewife called the police. From the victim's description and subsequent police artist's sketch, the police were able to recognize the face. It was their old friend, Albert DeSalvo, the Measuring Man.

Since they were investigating the more serious Boston Strangler case, the Cambridge police called DeSalvo and invited him to the police station for questioning. On November 3 Albert appeared on time at the station house. While he was busy denying the attack, the housewife from Cambridge was watching him through a two-way mirror in the interrogation room. She identified him instantly.

The police arrested DeSalvo and had him sent to Boston State Hospital at Bridgewater for observation while he was awaiting his trail. It never occurred to them that DeSalvo could have been the Boston Strangler because he did not fit the Strangler Bureau's psychological profile. He was married, he felt no special rage toward his mother, he wasn't impotent. Albert seemed to be just another sex offender.

Before his first court appearance DeSalvo started making cryptic remarks about the Strangler to his doctors at Bridgewater. As if passing a causal remark, Albert said the Strangler "should be studied, not buried." But the psychiatrists were not interested in DeSalvo's theories about the Strangler, after all, what could this petty sex offender know regarding these fiendish murders?

After a brief court appearance, Albert was remanded again to Boston State Hospital for a second evaluation. Whereas the first psychiatric evaluation stated DeSalvo was a borderline psychotic, but competent to stand trial, the second evaluation found him to be "potentially suicidal and clearly overtly schizophrenic." The doctors were divided whether DeSalvo was competent to stand trial. It was during this second period that Albert proclaimed himself to be the Boston Strangler.

F. Lee Bailey, famous defense attorney, takes time out to read a book about one of his famous cases. Although Bailey never defended De-Salvo in court for the Strangler killings, he negotiated the crucial immunity from prosecution deal between his client and Assistant Attorney General John S. Bottomley.

Albert DeSalvo's life term in Walpole State Prison, Massachusetts was abruptly cut short by three inmates who stabbed him to death. This picture is of an unidentified weeping woman leaving the funeral. No one seemed to know her identity.

No one listened to the babbling patient for close to two weeks. Then a few of the staff thought perhaps this man should be taken seriously. Psychiatrist Robert Mezer spent some time with DeSalvo and was convinced that his patient was the Strangler.

At the DeSalvo trial for the Green Man attacks Dr. Mezer startled the court by disclosing some of the information that the defendant told him. But under Massachusetts' law a doctor who obtains information from a suspect in a case cannot enter it as evidence at the trial. So Mezer's comments were stricken from the record, and because there were no reporters in the courtroom covering this low level crime, the full story never came out at the time.

Bottomley was in the middle of a quandary, on one hand he wanted to bring DeSalvo to justice and on the hand he wanted to close the Boston Strangler case. Since the only testimony that could close the case was Albert's, and he was not going to give it freely, Bottomley had to make a deal with DeSalvo's lawyer, F. Lee Bailey.

In July 1965 Albert met with Bottomley under the conditions set by Bailey; in essence, nothing that DeSalvo said could ever be used against him in a court of law. Originally the interview was scheduled for about a half an hour. But a bond was formed between Bottomley and DeSalvo, and the first meeting lasted for five hours. It was like pricking a boil with a needle, once the putrid truth was let out there was no stopping it. In all, Bottomley's interviews comprised about 50 hours of tapes and 2,000 pages of transcripts. When the meetings were over the police verified all of Albert's details and were convinced that DeSalvo was the Boston Strangler.

The Boston Strangler was never sent to prison for his crimes, but in 1967 Albert DeSalvo was given a life sentence for rape and armed robbery in the Green Man attacks. Six years after he was sent to Walpole State Prison, in Massachusetts, DeSalvo was found dead in his cell. He was stabbed 16 times by three inmates, allegedly in a dispute over drugs, although some believe he was killed just for being the Boston Strangler.

As many other famous murder cases which do not have a tidy ending, there are some who believe DeSalvo was not the Boston Strangler. The doubters point to the lack of corroborating evidence and the fact that DeSalvo was never brought to trial for the murders as a strong indication, if not proof, that there were holes in Albert's story. Nevertheless the case is listed as closed by the Massachusetts attorney general's office.

1966
The Killer and the Hero: Charles Whitman

Charles Whitman looked like the All-American boy. He was friendly, caring and good with children. The last quality was noticed by the parents of many Boy Scouts. Scouting was in his blood, having been an exemplary eagle scout during his youth. Later he joined the Marines and distinguished himself by achieving the class of sharpshooter. Many believed Whitman's military career was as distinguished as his childhood and teenage scouting experiences. This is only the partial truth. Although he was quickly promoted to the rank of corporal because of his attention to duties, he was just as quickly demoted to private for such infractions as assault, gambling and the illegal possession of firearms. After his honorable discharge from the Marines Whitman enrolled at the University of Texas in Austin where he maintained a B average as an architectural engineering major.

A few minutes past midnight on August 1 Whitman stared at the 307-foot campus tower from the top floor of his house. He was suffering an extreme bout of depression and the tower shown like beacon in the hot and heavy black night. Charles felt the tower tug at him, draw his darkest fantasies from some inner crevasse of his soul. It compelled that hidden part of him to come forth and vent its murderous fury upon the world.

Whatever options he had evaporated an hour after he killed his mother. It was better that way. She had suffered too many disappointments and too many beatings in her life. Now his father had left her. He told himself he had killed her so she would not face the disgrace he was about to bring upon the family. He was puzzled over why he felt he had to shoot her in the head after he had already killed her with a knife.

Later that evening his wife came home and Whitman killed her too. She was laid out comfortably on the the bed, hands fold across her chest. Two typewritten notes were left on his desk. The first contained a bizarre request. "I am prepared to die. After my death, I wish an autopsy to be performed on me to see if there is any mental disorder." The second was a recitation of his deeds. "12:00 a.m.—Mother dead, 3 o' clock—both dead, " with a penciled postscript, "Life is not worth living. "

Austin police officer Ramiro Martinez was not in a good mood, in fact he was angry. Before leaving the stationhouse he learned that he was denied the prized promotion to sergeant. He had worked hard for the promotion, but excellence was not the only criteria under consideration. In 1966 advancement for Latinos in the Austin Police Department was slow to nonexistent. Yet law enforcement was in his blood and, except for a few senior officers, many thought him to be a superior police officer and a born leader.

As he lay in bed he furiously pondered the future, what he should do next—changing jobs even though his wife was expecting a baby in a few months or leaving police work altogether were two options. His personal credo was, if you had a job to do, you did your best. That was the only way to make changes in the system. Yet he was hurt by the failure to make sergeant. And so these thoughts kept turning over and over in his brain until he fell into a fitful sleep. Tomorrow he was off duty and he had all day to think. But Ramiro had no way of knowing that tomorrow he would be a hero.

The dawn's rising sun announced another hot, steamy day. Whitman packed his Marine footlocker into his pickup truck and went shopping. He was in the market for ammunition, and a really high powered rifle. He was buying his dream, his nightmarish vision of an avenging angel raining death and misery from on high. Sweat, from heat and anticipation, stained his T-shirt.

Sell, sell, sell, the gun shop owner did not know when to stop. Not that he was sorry; the young man bought a couple of rifles and enough ammo to carry on a small war. The kid was probably a very avid hunter. But the owner loved to talk about guns; the young man just wanted to leave with his purchases.

117

Kathleen and Charles J. Whitman looked like a happy "Ameri-can" couple on their August 17, 1962 wedding day. Four years later Whitman would kill Kathleen, his mother and 16 strangers.

Once his armaments were complete, Whitman drove to the university and parked his truck. Hauling the footlocker was easy because he had the foresight to tie it to a hand-truck. No one noticed him as he rode the elevator to the 27th floor. The receptionist sitting behind her desk by the elevator questioned Whitman, and he answered her by bashing her head in with his rifle butt.

For the next few moments events unfolded rapidly. Their exact sequence is unclear. Whitman dragged his footlocker, still loaded on the hand-truck, up a stairwell to the tower observation deck. He was closely followed by a group of tourists. Two of the sightseers were cut down by shot blasts and the surviving members of the group ran shrieking back to the 27th floor. They found a small room at the end of the hall and hid there.

At some point before the shooting of the tourists and after Whitman's arrival on the deck level, he was seen unpacking his weapons by two campus security guards. They had been alerted to his presence by someone who witnessed him going up the stairs. The man on the deck had his back to the door so the campus security guards quietly returned to the stairwell unseen. They were unarmed and no match for this walking army. No one noticed the receptionist's body at this time. The chief of campus security notified the Austin Police that they had an armed intruder on the observation deck. About this time Whitman jammed the deck door shut with the hand-truck.

Having a nut perched in a high place armed with

Whitman shown with his mother, father, and brothers John (left), and Patrick (right). A few years after this picture was taken Whitman's father would leave his wife and move to Florida.

some rifles is always a dangerous situation, but the police sent only two squad cars to investigate. After all it was a college campus and the tower had previously been the focus of a few pranks. In the back of the assignment officer's mind may have been the thought that even if this was not a practical joke, who could hit anything from that distance?

Whitman took aim. It was 11:40 a.m. and most of the students were in class. He had been delayed 10 minutes by killing the receptionist and the tourists.

Those few moments were the difference between a sea of crawling targets and several dozen or so strolling groups.

Crack, crack, the sounds of faraway pops were heard as six students walked across the campus lawn. Two of them jerked slightly and fell, one boy dead, one girl badly wounded. A small crowd gathered. They didn't have the faintest idea what was going on. Someone noticed that they were shot, and someone else noticed the boy was dead. The group

One of several photos found after Whitman was killed. Police assumed this photograph was taken within a week of Whitman's killing spree.

Mrs. Edna Townsley, an elevator operator in the University Tower and Dr. Robert H. Boyer, mathematics professor at the university were two of Whitman's sniping victims.

Austin police officers futilely attempt to shoot Whitman on the University Tower. Most of the police rifles did not have the range to reach the sniper and those that did have the range were inaccurate at that distance.

Police bullets kick up masonry dust around the University of Texas clock tower. None of the ground fire hit Whitman during his 90 minute sniping spree.

An aerial view of the University of Texas in Austin where Charles Whitman shot 46 people from the clock tower. The silhouetted bodies show the approximate location of the victims.

froze for a moment, uncomprehending, staring up at the sky.

Whitman turned his attention toward the main entrance of one of the campus buildings. This time he missed, and the sound of bullets ricocheting and hitting the concrete broadcast the rain of death from the tower. Everyone who heard them scattered, seeking shelter from the sniper.

A young man two blocks away was walking down a commercial avenue, unaware of the commotion on the university campus, unaware of the dying; a second later he was permanently unaware of anything. A bullet shot from a high powered rifle ended his life. Store windows shattered. Bystanders ducked for cover. Bullet holes appeared in car hoods. Panic gripped the area and everyone started running from the tower and the pointed death seeking any victim.

Three blocks away two men heard the first news report on a passing car radio. One man turned to his friend and said, "We're three blocks away. He can't reach us." Five seconds later he was shot dead getting into his pickup truck.

From on high everybody looked so small. Most men would have had trouble hitting a car, let alone a human being, but not Charles Whitman, Marine sharpshooter. Over and above the advantage of a telescopic sight on his rifle, he was a really great shot. There were at least 20 people by now bearing mute and moaning witness to his accuracy.

Ramiro Martinez first heard reports of the shooting on his kitchen radio. The newscast interrupted Martinez's preoccupation with his future. As he listened intently, his spouse began to worry. She was a policeman's wife and her greatest fear was that one

A terrified young woman takes refuge behind a statue, while a wounded man lies on the grass (left) near by. Tom Lankes, the photographer, took this picture while bullets whizzed all around him. It was one of the first photos taken and the scene and the most widely published at the time.

day she would get a phone call telling her Ramiro was killed in the line of duty. Now she watched as he changed into his uniform. Pleading with him didn't help, but she tried anyway. Even though it was his day off, his sense of duty would not allow him to listen to the radio while his fellow officers were being shot. He called the stationhouse and they told him to report to the campus. Martinez turned to his wife and with a smile said all headquarters wanted him to do was direct traffic from the area. Watching him walk to he car, his wife somehow knew he was lying.

Headquarters didn't know what to do. The Austin Police Force never had an experience such as this. Many patrolmen called in on their car radios and likened the situation to a war zone. Hospitals were overflowing with gunshot victims, people were still panicking in the streets, traffic was a mess, the wounded lay on the ground in need of rescue, policemen were getting shot and the FBI wanted to get

in on the act. The first action the police took to restore order was to set up an on-site emergency command-post near the campus, but not within sight of the tower.

When the firing started several men grabbed their rifles from their cars and trucks. They set up a firing line behind a stone wall and extending beyond to several tall, thick trees. Volley after volley was fired at the man in the tower. A few had rifles that could reach the tower, but no one had the skill to hit the sniper. The bullets kept raining down and finding their targets.

Ramiro drove to the campus. A few blocks away he met one of his fellow officers helping a wounded patrolman into an ambulance. To his dismay Martinez discovered no one was in charge. The scattered policemen were out of contact with the command-post being set up a few blocks away. It was up to each of them to do something. Ramiro left his car and decided to get closer to the tower on foot.

A dazed Ramiro Martinez just after he killed Whitman in a shoot out on the University of Texas clock tower. First reports from the scene said that Martinez was wounded; these later proved to be untrue.

The radio blared the confusion Charles had wrought. Between his murderous shooting sprees Whitman listened intently to the newscasts describing the campus in chaos. He had prepared well. Transistor radio, water-canteens, candy bars, toilet paper and plenty of ammunition were laying about within easy reach. Killing made Charles thirsty, and when he drank the water he felt hungry. Eating the candy bars sent sugar jolting to his brain. It was like a numbing bolt of energy that made him want to jump up, aim and kill again.

There was this one cop who ran a broken field, from tree to statue to bushes. Every so often, when Whitman got him in sight, the officer would brake right or left and was gone. He looked like the same guy Charles had seen through his scope a few blocks away. The cop appeared to be running towards the tower. He had already helped to carry two wounded people to safety and calmed at least a half dozen more. After he did what had to be done, Martinez kept running his broken field toward the tower.

Seeking to resolve the crisis quickly, someone in the police command post had the bright idea of sending a police marksman past the tower in a crop-dusting biplane. For several minutes the scene resembled something out of King Kong, except in this case the target on the building was shooting back. The attempt failed because the tower sniper was able to put more bullets in the biplane than the marksman could put inside the tower. Neither the owner/pilot nor the marksman wanted to be shot down by the madman.

Martinez made a mad dash for a building adjacent to the tower while the sniper was engaged with the biplane. Inside he found a group of panicky civilians asking him to take them to safety. It took a while for Ramiro to convince the people that they were safer inside, on the ground floor of the building, than anywhere outside, where there was not adequate cover for such a large group.

A short run and a few shots later Martinez made it to the tower. There he met up with some of his fellow policemen who had taken an underground short cut. All attempts to reach the command post were thwarted by busy phone lines. It was up to the small group of police officers to get the sniper.

Some fellow patrolmen outside the tower spotted Martinez's group in the lobby. Although they could not communicate with the tower group they did inform the command post that there was a contingent of police going up to the observation deck. The command-post in turn let this bit of news out to reporters in an effort to let everyone know the police were doing their best. The reporters phoned the story in to their various news desks, and the broad-cast media announced the policemen's presence on radio and television.

Maybe Whitman really was waiting for the police to deliver him from his torment. Now that he heard they were coming for him on his radio, and that it was only a matter of time, he switched his attention from firing at the population below to waiting for the police attack.

Patrolmen Houston McCoy, Jerry Day and Martinez reached the 27th floor by using the service elevator. They were accompanied by Allen Crum, a campus bookstore manager who knew the building. Crum guided McCoy and Day through the underground connecting tunnel. By sheer oversight, Martinez was not introduced to Crum and assumed, because Crum was wearing a suit and carrying a rifle, that he was a detective.

The group split up. McCoy and Day escorted the remaining tourists hiding on the 27th floor downstairs. Martinez and Crum went up the stairwell to the deck. It was here that Ramiro deputized Crum when he learned that Allen was not a law enforcement officer.

It was a judgement call. Martinez decided to force the door to the roof and get the sniper without waiting for McCoy and Day. He felt that every moment he waited increased the chances of some else on the ground getting shot.

The hand-truck fell with a clattering sound as the deck door was flung open. After such a racket, surprising the sniper was out of the question. Martinez crept around the deck in one direction and Crum went in the other. Every nerve in Ramiro's body was tingling, every muscle was ready for action as he eased himself forward, around the tower. McCoy and Day quietly joined Martinez. Inch by inch the trio moved around the corner toward the sniper. They had only one more side of the tower to go.

Whitman heard a noise and turned to face it. Martinez moved away from the wall and pointed his revolver at the sniper. Whitman was startled; he was facing in the wrong direction. It was Crum the sniper heard and not the policemen. It was taking Whitman an agonizingly long time to swing his rifle toward Martinez. Ramiro saw Whitman move and pulled the trigger, again and again. Each report was followed by another. The sniper's body jerked several times and was still. He never got off a shot.

It took awhile to notify the people on the ground that the sniper was dead. Every time someone waved from the deck, the hunters below fired at them. Finally word reached the command post and all the shooting stopped.

Within an hour of the sniper's death the people of Austin knew Whitman's story. From beginning to

Charles A. Whitman, father of the sniper, answering questions from reporters about his son. Behind Whitman senior one of his other sons, Patrick Whitman and his wife.

The bullet riddled body of Charles J. Whitman after Ramiro Martinez put an end to his killing spree.

Whitman came prepared to wage war. Pictured are the rifles, pistols and ammunition the sniper took with him to the observation deck of the tower.

end the whole incident took 96 minutes. The casualties numbered 46 people shot, 16 killed and 30 wounded, not counting Whitman's mother and wife.

An autopsy revealed that Whitman had a walnut-sized, malignant tumor in the hypothalamus area of the brain. At the time many believed this might have been the cause of his murderous shooting spree. Since then medical experts have changed their minds. They do not believe that the presence of the tumor could have caused his bizarre behavior.

Martinez, McCoy and Day were awarded the Austin Police Medal of Honor. Allen Crum was awarded Texas' highest civilian medal. Shortly after the tower incident Ramiro Martinez left the Austin Police Force to become a Texas Ranger.

1970
Acid Made Me Do It: Dale Merle Nelson

He was a family man. Except for his infrequent drinking sprees, Dale Nelson was an okay guy. At 31 years old, he lived with his wife and three children in West Creston, British Columbia. Their wooden shack was located at the end of a dirt road surrounded by a wilderness of bushes. He wasn't a rich man. Nelson made a living doing freelance logging work, when it was available.

His neighbors knew him, but not well. He was the kind of guy who just got by. No one thought that Dale would ever do anything great, or anything bad. Twice, when Nelson fell into a deep depression and went on a drinking binge, he hit his wife. She suffered a bruise on both occasions. But these were isolated incidences, and not indicative of his general behavior or attitude.

His alcoholic bouts usually began with Nelson becoming despondent. His feelings of sexual inadequacy grew to overwhelming proportions. To blanket these feelings, to lift himself from the depths of worthlessness, he would drink. It was said that Nelson could drink 10 men under the table during one of these binges and still walk a straight line.

On September 4, 1970 Dale Nelson went on another drinking spree. It started at noon and went on till midnight. In those 12 hours he consumed whiskey, beer, wine and brandy. Where he consumed the alcohol was immaterial to Nelson, as long as he kept drinking. He was seen drunk bars, hotels, motel, bowling alleys and liquor stores, alone and with friends.

Shortly after midnight he drove to Maureen McKay's house. Nelson expected his cousin-in-law, recently separated from her husband and raising a 4-year-old daughter on her own, to be alone. She wasn't. She had a male friend over and they were sitting on a sofa in the living room, talking. Neither McKay nor her friend noticed Nelson enter the house and then leave.

Next he went to Mrs. Shirley Wasyks' house, another relative by marriage. Finding that her husband was at a logging camp and that she was alone with her three daughters, aged 12, eight and seven, Nelson beat her to death. Fists were the only implement Dale used to pound the life out of Shirley. The children were in the corner shrieking, unable to help their mother. Nelson then turned his attention to 7-year-old Tracey. He grabbed her by the neck, and squeezed. Tracey struggled for only a minute before she died.

Not content with killing only the little girl, Nelson cut her open from the groin to the heart. A black madness fed on Dale's brain as he ripped open his victim's stomach and ate her undigested food. His next victim was screaming eight-year-old Sharlene, who was luckier than her younger sister. Nelson only raped her. Coming to her senses, Darlene, the oldest sister, escaped from the house and ran for help. Dale was occupied with Sharlene and did not notice that Darlene was missing.

Having had his fill of relatives, Nelson went to the nearby home of Ray Phipps. He didn't know his neighbor at all. Dale may have spoken all of 10 words to the man and his family during the last year. Ray no sooner opened his door than Nelson shot him dead with a rifle.

In rapid succession Isabelle St. Amand, Ray's common law wife, and her four children, were shot, knifed and clubbed to death. Still hungry for more cruelty, Nelson carried the dying eight-year-old Cathy St. Amend into the wild shrub land and raped her.

A patrol car was sent to the Wasyks' house in response to Darlene's hysterical fit at a neighbor's home. The officers were utterly horrified by the carnage they encountered. Thinking that nothing else could happen at the murder site, they went off to search the area for Sharlene and Nelson. Ten minutes later they found her wandering in the brush.

From his hiding place close to the house, Nelson watched the police leave the Wasyks' home. He crept back inside and stole Tracey's dead and mutilated body. Driven by forces beyond his understanding, Dale further desecrated the girl's body in the brush land. An hour later, all that was left of Tracey Wasyks was a torso, minus a heart and genitals. Her legs and arms were strewn about. Later that night the police found most of Tracey 40 feet from Nelson's car.

The manhunt for Dale Nelson lasted a day and a half. In the end he gave himself up. He had cooperated with police who were searching for Cathy St. Amend's body. No one ever found Tracey Wasyks' missing organs.

At his trial Nelson admitted everything, but added a new wrinkle to his defense. The blame for all his abhorrent behavior was attributed to a drug, "It must have been the LSD." In fact those were the first words he spoke when he was arrested. Nelson's defense attorney attempted to show that his client was insane.

The jury believed none of his excuses. All they needed to hear was the testimony from the surviving Wasyks sisters to find him guilty. Dale Nelson was sentenced to life imprisonment.

1975
Jimmy Hoffa Where Oh Where Has His Body Gone?

For decades James R. Hoffa was a controversial union leader with strong ties to organized crime. From 1957 to 1971 he was president of the International Brotherhood of Teamsters. On July 30, 1975 his past and present collided, and he vanished.

The son of a coal driller, Hoffa was born on February 14, 1913 in Brazil, Indiana. His father died when he was seven years old and the family moved to Detroit in 1924. Hoffa quit school at the age of 14 to help support his mother and brothers, working as a stock boy and warehouseman. In the thirtiess he began his union organizing career as a business agent for Local 299 in Detroit.

Union organizing was rough business during the Depression. Business agents were killed, cars were bombed and Hoffa's brother was shot. "Three different times someone broke into the office and destroyed our furniture. Cars would crowd us off the streets. Then it got worse. They hired thugs who were out to get us, and brother, your life was in your hands every day. There was only one way to survive—fight back."

It was during these union organizing activities that Hoffa rubbed shoulders with gangsters. Sometimes they fought with him, sometimes against him. But in the end Hoffa won his battles with management by being better at making deals with the mobsters. It was simple, the Teamsters wouldn't get into organized crime and organized crime would maintain a hands off attitude with the Teamsters. This agreement quickly spread across the country.

By 1940 Hoffa had become chairman of the Central States Drivers Council. In 1942 he was president of the Michigan Conference of Teamsters and finally, in 1957, he became an international president. Much of his rise within the union was due to his reputation in the trucking industry as a tough and knowledgeable negotiator.

As an international president Hoffa centralized union administration and bargaining, and played a key role in creating the first national freight hauling agreement. He helped to make the Teamsters the largest labor union in America. So where did he go wrong?

Not all of his methods were legal. Occasionally he would extort money from firms hiring Teamsters by threatening a strike or bodily harm. Other times he would bribe government officials, launder money or loan certain mobsters money from the Teamster pension funds. He was guilty of racketeering.

Up until the sixties many law enforcement officials yearned to put Hoffa behind bars; none were successful. Then came the United States attorney general from 1961-1964, Robert F. Kennedy, President Kennedy's brother. Jimmy Hoffa finally met his match. Kennedy first took notice of Hoffa in 1957 as chief council to the McClellan Committee, officially known as the Senate Select Committee on Improper Activities in the Labor or Management Field.

"Get Hoffa" became a top priority when Robert Kennedy became attorney general. In 1961 Kennedy appeared on *Johnny Carson's Tonight Show* for 10 minutes, solely to announce the beginning of his campaign. One year later Kennedy's tireless efforts resulted in Hoffa's arrest and trial for extortion from firms hiring Teamsters. The case ended with a hung jury, but Hoffa was arrested for bribing one of the jurors. This time he was found guilty and sentenced to eight years in prison. Hoffa's woes didn't end there. In 1964 he was convicted of misappropriation of Teamster pension funds. His lawyers used every legal trick and appeal to get their client out of

Jimmy Hoffa, controversial former Teamster Union leader, left his house one morning and disappeared. There is no doubt that he was murdered. It is believed that his rumored links to organized crime led him to an untimely death and an unmarked grave.

John Kennedy was the United States Senator from Massachusetts in 1957, while his brother was the chief counsel to the McClellan Committee. The two men often conferred on committee matters. Occasionally Hoffa was the target of their investigations.

Robert Kennedy (standing), who would later become the United
States Attorney General and prosecute Jimmy Hoffa, first took notice
of the Teamster leader during the 1957 Senate Select Committee on
Improper Activities in Labor or Management Field. This committee
was popularly called the McClellan Committee.

Certain elements in organized crime believe that Hoffa had obtained copies of the Teamsters' accounting books and had sent a trusted "bookkeeper" to a hotel in Phoenix, Arizona to review them. The unofficial audit produced just the information that Hoffa needed to regain control of the union. But the mob suspected something was up and reacted quickly. When the bookkeeper heard of Hoffa's disappearance he burned his copies of the books and vanished.

Sean Landeta (right), kicker for the New York Giants, commented upon hearing the rumor that Jimmy Hoffa might be buried under the goal post in the Meadowlands stadium, "I guess it gives a whole new meaning to kicking into the coffin corner."

prison. They lost and in 1967 Hoffa began serving his sentences, which totaled 13 years. Always the fighter, Hoffa and his followers convinced President Nixon, in 1971, to commute his sentence with the proviso that he would not engage in union activity for 10 years.

As soon as he was released Hoffa plotted to regain control of the union from his former friend and protégé, Frank Fitzsimmons. Fitzsimmons had the backing of an organized crime boss who found him much easier to get along with than Hoffa. The mob figured that Fitzsimmons was seen as clean by the White House, while Hoffa was viewed as a pardoned former felon. Should Hoffa succeed in regaining control of the Teamsters, the FBI would begin scrutinizing union activities with a microscope. That would not be good for business, mob business that is. Hoffa was told to take a hike, but he proved to be "hard of hearing and kept coming on."

On July 30, 1975, Hoffa went to the Manchus Red Fox restaurant in suburban Detroit to meet with Anthony "Tony Pro" Provenzano, a New Jersey Teamster and a suspected Mafia captain, Anthony Giacalone, a Detroit mob figure, and a third man identified as a Detroit labor leader. Both Provenzano and Giacalone claimed they never showed up for the meeting. Instead, Hoffa was picked up at 2:45 p.m. by several men in a maroon Mercury sedan. He was never seen again.

One version states that Hoffa was shot shortly after entering the auto and his body was disposed of at a mob-owned sanitation company in Hantramck, Michigan. A variation of this theme has Hoffa gar-

roted and his body put through a mob-owned fat rendering plant. The factory later burned down and arson was the suspected cause of the fire.

The FBI believe they know who did it and why, but they lack sufficient evidence to gain convictions. A successful prosecution would require testimony of one of the participants, and there is very little chance of that happening. Technically the case is still open, with one FBI agent assigned to it. And quite a large case it is, filling 12 filing cabinets. All is not lost, however. Law enforcement authorities believe that almost everyone involved eventually went to prison for other crimes, and the Hoffa investigation has led to other successful prosecutions.

Recently Donald "Tony the Greek" Frankos, a federally protected mob witness, added a humorous wrinkle to the Hoffa story. He stated in the November 1989 issue of *Playboy* magazine that poor old Jimmy was shot in a house near Detroit, not in the maroon Mercury sedan. Afterwards, Hoffa's body was cut into large pieces and stored in a freezer for five months before being packed in an oil drum. The drum was shipped to New Jersey and buried near the west end-zone of Giants Stadium at the Meadowlands in East Rutherford, which was under construction at the time.

Meadowlands officials deny that an oil drum packed with body parts was found when the field at Giants Stadium was replaced in 1989. But Jets and Giants fans have found the idea of Hoffa being buried in the stadium quite funny. As Giants punter Sean Landeta once said, "I guess it gives a whole new meaning to kicking into the coffin corner."

1986
No Body, No Crime: The Woodchipper Murder

It was a telephone bill that caused Helle Crafts murder. If she hadn't pursued the matter at hand she might have still been alive today.

Thirty-nine years old, tall with ash blond hair, attractive and smart, Helle Crafts believed in late July 1986 that her marriage was coming to an end. Both she and her and husband, Richard, were employed by different companies in the air travel business. Helle worked as a flight attendant for Pan Am and Richard was a pilot for Eastern. Their schedules were such that for days at a time neither one was home to care for their children, Andrew, 10, Thomas, eight, and Kristina, five. At such times their nanny, Marie Thomas, took care of the children.

The Crafts lived in Newtown, Connecticut, a small, quiet town 10 miles east of Danbury. It was a difficult marriage and Richard was not a very communicative person. Most of Helle's friends thought him a bit odd, a loner, a man who was more comfortable with his gun collection, making his own bullets and puttering around his basement than he was with human beings. His other activities included drinking one or two six packs of beer a day and part time jobs with the Newtown police department and various security firms.

Crafts spent 10 years in the military from 1956-66. Some of the time was spent in the Marines as a pilot, and the rest of the time he flew for the CIA's Air America. After a few short stints as a fire fighter, helicopter pilot and aerial photographer, he joined Eastern as a highly qualified airman. In 1984 Richard had been operated on for colon cancer. After more than a year of treatment he returned to work while still undergoing chemotherapy. By July 1986 he had stopped the chemotherapy and the cancer remained in remission.

Early in 1986 Helle was routinely checking the phone bills for Marie Thomas' long distance calls

when Richard entered the room and roughly took them out of her hands. "I'll take care of these," he said and the phone bills never came to the house again. Richard's unusual action made Helle suspicious. After a few months, Helle investigated the disappearance of bills with the local phone company. She found out that they were being sent to a post office box in another section of Newtown. By sheer coincidence Helle had a box in the same post office. It was one she shared with her friend, Rita Buonanno, for their part-time curtain business. Helle charmed a post office worker into giving her the latest phone bill.

There was one New Jersey number that kept appearing on the phone bill. Helle dialed the number and got an answering machine recording belonging to "Nancy." Helle began to plot her husband's flights on the calendar. Since Richard never told her his schedule she put check marks next to the days he claimed to have been flying. No matter how Helle added it up, Crafts was away more than the 84 hour maximum allowed by the Eastern contract. Her worst suspicions about Richard's infidelities now seemed to be substantiated by fact, and she felt moved to take action.

On September 4 Helle met with Dianne Andersen, a well known and busy Connecticut divorce lawyer. Andersen routinely ascertained the couple's financial status. Richard earned $87,000 between his two jobs and Helle made $32,000 between her salary and her share of the curtain business. In round figures Andersen estimated that Helle could expect about $30,000 in alimony and child support.

Connecticut has no-fault divorce laws. Yet with proof of adultery, alcoholism or abuse the injured spouse would have a stronger case in court and would most likely receive a proper alimony and child support settlement. Adultery looked as if it was

Everyone liked Helle Crafts and none of her friends liked her husband, Richard. When Helle disappeared her friends thought his indifference was suspicious, but after a couple of weeks of insensitive behavior they were ready to believe the worst. They had yet to find out how fiendish Richard really was.

going to be the easiest case to prove. Andersen called Keith Mayo, a private detective whom she often hired in connection with such cases.

Thirty-four years old, six feet tall and beginning to find out that each day's activities did not burn all of his caloric intake, Mayo had been in the gum-shoe trade for six years. During this course of time he had learned a trick or two and made a few valuable contacts. One of these was Dave, a computer hacker, who could find the name and address to any phone number in the United States. Although Mayo never personally met Dave, he knew the hacker's work was flawless. Dave charged his clients $40 per number and Mayo marked the price up to $100.

Andersen called the private detective and requested the name and address for the New Jersey number on Crafts' bill. In less than 20 minutes Mayo returned her call with the name, Nancy Dodd, and a street address in Middletown, New Jersey. Dodd worked as a flight attendant, but unlike Helle, she worked for Eastern. Ironically, Helle remembered meeting Nancy Dodd several years before.

Now it was all but certain that Richard Crafts was guilty of adultery, but the court would need proof. Helle, at Andersen's recommendation, hired Mayo to stake out Dodd's house in New Jersey. The evidence to be used in court would come in the form of verbal and photographic testimony. There was also an outside chance that the photos would force Richard Crafts to settle out of court.

As per Mayo's instructions, Helle paid close attention to her husband's flight calendar for the month of September. When Richard's schedule seemed to be going over his allowed hours, Helle found some pretext to call the airline and check his actual return. Sure enough, he was arriving on September 21 and not on September 22 as he had told her.

Mayo received a phone call from Helle telling the private eye of Richard's "missing" day. Mayo already knew Dodd's general description and the make of her car along with the license plate number of Crafts' 1985 LTD Crown Victoria. This LTD model was a favorite among many of the nation's state police troops. September 21 was a Sunday. Mayo had a busy schedule the next day. This trip he would only check to see if the errant husband was shacking up with Dodd. If this was true he would come back a second time to secure the crucial photos.

As the private detective had expected, he found both cars parked outside Nancy Dodd's split level condo. He and his associate stayed just long enough to see the lights go out and no one leave. This would establish that Crafts had spent the night with his New Jersey bedmate.

A week later Richard had another "missing day" and again the pilot went straight to Nancy's waiting arms. This time Mayo was waiting. Once more both cars were parked in front of the condo. This time Mayo and his associate would stay all night, talking, dozing, waiting.

Their wait ended at 9:30 a.m. when the lovers emerged holding hands. Both detectives were armed with cameras as well as guns. He was a part-time policeman and kept a gun in his car. There was always a chance that Crafts would spot Mayo and his associate snapping pictures like under-employed fashion photographers. Would he shoot them under these circumstances, Mayo wondered. For five minutes the couple hugged and kissed outside by their parked cars. Then for no particular reason Nancy looked up and right at them. Their eyes met. But as lovers often do, she was looking without seeing. Nothing short of a 500 pound gorilla would have gotten her attention.

The photos cut into her like a knife and Helle's tears rolled down her face in a steady stream when she saw them. It was at that very moment that she decided to divorce Richard. Yet she wanted to wait until the results of his medical examination were known. After all, if Richard was going to die soon, serving him with divorce papers would have been in bad taste. As it turned out Richard was given a clean bill of health.

The last time Andersen talked to Helle was on the telephone on October 14. Helle told the lawyer to go ahead with the divorce. A month later the papers were ready but they proved almost impossible to serve. Richard Crafts used one dodge after another to avoid receiving them. The game of legal hide and seek continued until Thanksgiving when the situation would change drastically.

Dianne Andersen remembered a few ominous notes in her discussions with Helle Crafts. One was the existence of Richard's gun collection, some were kept loaded in the basement. Even though it was possible to get the guns out of the house with a court order, Helle felt that the action would enrage her husband. She decided to take her chances with the guns in the house. The second note was something she said as she was leaving the lawyer's office. "If something happens to me, don't believe it was accidental." During her many years of experience Andersen had heard this statement from a small percentage of her clients. Nothing ever happened in those cases and she felt that the same would be true in Helle's case. Yet there was something about the manner in which the statement was said that made it stick in her memory.

Helle's lawyer did not know the hell the woman was going through. Her friends did. Each one had a piece of the picture. When added together the pieces produced a mosaic of an indecisive woman unbelieving of her husband's infidelity until the moment she saw the photos. And then there was no question that a divorce was in order. With the decision to divorce came the element of fear. Fear of a husband already feeling threatened with losing his job in the buy-out of Eastern Airlines by Texas Air; threatened with the loss of his mistress; threatened by his wife's legal action which might name his girl friend as a co-defendant; threatened by his close call with death; threatened by his whole world coming apart. Such a man, who had struck her in front of their friends once before, could conceivably kill her.

If she said it once she said it a dozen times during the two months before her death, "If something happens to me, don't believe it was accidental." When she was asked why she didn't just leave her husband, Helle said she was afraid Richard's police connections would track her down no matter where she went. She made the statement again to her friend and co-worker, Rita Buonanno, for the last time before her flight to Frankfurt. When they returned on the night of November 18, the air was heavy with an on-rushing snowstorm. Yet Helle's spirits were up. She was looking forward to having Thanksgiving with her children and some friends. The last person to see her alive, outside of her family, was a fellow flight attendant, Trudy Horvath. Helle said her last words to Trudy, as she was let out of the car. They were just a simple unemotional observation, "Richard's home."

Richard was home and was ready to put his gory plan in motion. You might say he had a pretty childish idea of what divorce meant to his well-being and a severe way of dealing with it. He prepared Helle's murder with a detailed eye for all the mechanical components. On October 29, Crafts purchased a 1980 VW Rabbit. He paid close to $800 over book value, but he didn't seem to mind. The car needed minor repairs and wasn't ready until November 17.

Helle found the hidden insurance receipt for the VW in early November and couldn't understand why Richard would need another car. In late November Richard would claim that he bought the new car because the housekeeper, Marie, had put too many dents in Helle's Tercel and his pickup truck. The police would surmise that he wanted the VW for Marie because he planned to leave the Tercel at the airport.

His next automotive purchase was a $15,000 Ford dump truck. It was a rather odd purchase. Although he said he needed it for spreading gravel on his driveway, he had it specially fitted with a hook for towing heavy equipment. If all Crafts wanted to

do was spread gravel he could have rented a truck at a fraction of the cost. But gravel was the last thing on his mind, moving a very specific piece of heavy equipment was the objective.

On November 13 Crafts traveled to Brewster, New York to buy a body-sized chest freezer, a shovel and pair of fireproof gloves. He paid cash for these items. After Richard bought the freezer, the salesman asked him for his name. Crafts told him he wasn't interested in the warranty; but he salesman persisted and Crafts finally told him to make the receipt out to Mr. Cash.

The next day Richard rented a large commercial woodchipper from Darien Rentals to be picked up on November 18. Crafts paid an extra $260 per day to insure that he would have the woodchipper on the day he needed it. The store owner told him it wasn't necessary to pay for the extra days because this machine, with a 12-inch log capacity, was not rented often, but Crafts insisted and finally the store owner relented.

The woodchipper, a Bush Bandit, is an industrial strength machine. Its main blade consists of a 2-inch thick disk with a 40-inch diameter. Attached to the disk are razor sharp 8-inch blades. Minced debris is ejected from a spout mounted on the rear by six fan blades. Depending on the arc of the spout the mechanism is capable of throwing material over 60 feet.

November 18, the day of the murder, Crafts unpacked the freezer while it was still in the cramped rear of the Toyota pickup. He hid the packing materials in the garage. The next step was crucial to his bloody design. He tested the freezer and it worked. If it hadn't, Helle might still be alive today. When night came, Richard parked the pickup behind the house and plugged in the freezer, setting it for -10 degrees. This last procedure is the converse of preheating an oven. It is to make sure that something is quickly frozen solid.

At 7 p.m., Helle arrived home tired after her long flight from Frankfurt, which was delayed for several hours. Richard had prepared dinner with an insincere aura of sweetness and light. The couple cleaned up the dishes together, and by 8 p.m. they were putting their children to bed. Andrew, the oldest, watched television for another half hour. The victim may have read her mail before preparing for bed. She had a busy day and was probably expecting to be asleep by 10 p.m. The victim had no idea how permanent that sleep would be.

It can be safely presumed Helle was turning back the covers of the bed about 10 p.m.. Unknown to the couple, it began to snow outside. Richard was holding a heavy object in his hands. It wasn't an obvious murder weapon such as an axe or sledge

It was difficult for the Newtown police to believe that one of their part-time police officers would be involved in the murder of his wife, let alone actually be the murderer.

*Most of the criminals that past through the Newtown Police Station
were accused of minor offenses. Murder was rare occurrence in the
small Connecticut town.*

hammer. It was something more innocuous—the 20-inch heavy police flashlight he kept recharging in the bathroom. Helle may have even seen it his hands and thought "there goes Richard playing with his toys." She was probably making the bed with her back to her husband when the first blow smashed her skull. As she turned toward Richard in disbelief of her situation, she was pounded again. This crushing blow opened a head wound, and head wounds bleed a lot. Helle fell onto the bed, her bleeding head grazing the side of the bed before she rolled to the floor. Unknown to Richard she smeared a six-inch bloody stripe on the mattress.

Richard's plans did not include Helle's bleeding. And bleed she did, all over the bedding and the bedroom rug. Oblivious to this complication, Crafts' first order of business was to prepare the body for disposal. According the plan this meant freezing. Rigidly adhering to his program, he carried the body, wrapped in a sheet or a blanket, downstairs to the waiting freezer in the Toyota pickup. He placed Helle inside the cold freezer already lined with plastic. Crafts was concerned with leaving the telltale hair or two in the freezer, but the liners were just the right item to deal with the unexpected blood. It didn't matter that he had to bend the body to make it fit, because he intended to cut it up later with a chain saw.

The best laid plans of murderers and mice often go astray. Crafts' timetable was now complicated by Helle's blood splattered all over the bedroom. Hastily he stripped the bed and took apart the bed frame, leaving the mattress resting on the floor. He cleaned up as best he could, although he decided to deal with the blood spot on the rug later. After temporarily storing the bedding and the bed frame in the garage, Crafts hid all of his wife's personal items, flight bags and passport in the closet.

Sometime around midnight Richard lay down on the mattress and pretended to be asleep. He was waiting for Marie to come home from her part-time job at McDonalds. It turned out to be a two-hour wait due to the the heavy snow. His timetable was definitely running late. At close to 3 a.m., when Richard was sure Marie was asleep, he sneaked out of the house and rolled Helle's Tercel down the driveway. When he was on the street he started the car and drove it someplace nearby where it would not be noticed.

It is almost certain that Crafts had to walk home in the snowstorm. Unknown to the busy Richard, an electrical transformer in Bethel had blown out at 3 a.m. At 3:44 a.m. the ripple effect on the power-grid blacked out the Crafts' home and the surrounding area. But Crafts called his brother-in-law, David Rogers, at 4:44 a.m. to check if the power was off in Westport. This call showed his ignorance of the extent of the blackout and when it had occurred. Richard made arrangements to bring Marie and his children by should the blackout continue into the early morning.

The next hour was spent in even more frenzied activity. Quietly he drove the pickup around to the garage door which faces the street. He unloaded the freezer, checked his Honda generator and drove across his snow-covered lawn to the kitchen door. Quickly the bedding and bed frame were loaded into the pickup. Richard drove to an unknown destination, perhaps to his other property on Currituck Road, and hid the bed frame and bedding.

At 6:00 a.m. Crafts woke up Marie and his children, informing them that the power was out and he would drive them to his sister's house in Westport, where they would stay until the power returned. Under no circumstances could they stay in the house since there was no heat. He completely ignored the fact that he could have used the fireplace or his kerosene lanterns for heat.

After a quick breakfast the group was ushered through the rarely used front door and down the slippery, ice-covered steps. Usually the Crafts went from the kitchen, through the garage, and into a car. Marie noted that the Tercel she had driven home the night before was missing. But she could not figure out how it was driven past the pickup truck and Ford Crown Victoria blocking the driveway.

Without warning five-year-old Kristina started walking back to the house, announcing that she was going to get her mittens. In one unexpected movement Crafts lifted his daughter up and roughly deposited her into the cab of the pickup. Kristina began to cry. Richard ignored his daughter's wails and started out in his car for Karen and David Rogers' house in Westport.

There was no rest for the weary murderer. Crafts fixed pancakes for his children at the Rogers' house and by 9 a.m. he was out doing errands. Without a moment to spare he purchased some kerosene and deposited a $300 check made out to Helle. He raced to call the Rogers at noon and tell them the power was still out. This was a lie. The power was restored in his area at 10:44 a.m., but there was no way for Crafts to know this; he wasn't home at the time. Next it was off to the shopping plaza to buy replacement bedding, then call the Rogers again at 3:00 p.m. to inform them the electricity was on, and then race home to move the pickup containing the generator, and Helle's body inside the freezer, to his other property.

At some point during the busy day Crafts made a

decision to keep the generator running inside the rear cab of the pickup. He had to be sure that the body in the freezer was frozen solid. It would not do to have any soft spots inside the body when he used the chain-saw to cut it into log-sized pieces. If it wasn't solid the soft tissue would spatter and might cause Crafts problems if it was discovered.

Still Richard's work was not done. He had to find time to move his wife's Toyota Tercel to a shopping center in Danbury, where it would not be noticed for a day or so. This feat was a tribute to Crafts' military logistical ability. Not only did he have to hide the car, but he had to find some way to return to his house. This was when the VW Rabbit entered into the grand scheme of things.

After parking Helle's Tercel, Richard picked up the car he previously bought in Danbury. He drove the new auto to his Currituck Road property and hid it. After a few days he would park the car by his house. This was the very same car described on the insurance receipt that Helle found in early November. Too bad she wasn't around to find out that her suspicions were wrong. It was not a present for Nancy Dodd; it was purchased for her murder.

The other vehicle used in the plan was not ready as scheduled. Crafts had wanted to pick up the Ford dump truck, with the specially fitted hook, on Wednesday, November 19. Early Tuesday he was told it was not going to be ready. This must have been on his mind as he drove his children home from Westport late that evening. He needed the truck to haul the woodchipper and he needed the woodchipper to atomize Helle's body. Crafts was already a day behind schedule.

Thursday started off with more problems. First the truck still wasn't ready when Richard started calling at 9:10 a.m. This situation was not remedied until well past noon. Crafts had to accept a U-Haul rental to tow his woodchipper. He cringed at the thought of showing up at Darien Rentals with a bright yellow and white U-Haul. He was right. The owner at Darien Rentals had never seen anyone pick up an industrial strength woodchipper with a rental truck. It was just not done.

The second problem came in the form of Helle's friend and co-worker, Rita Buonanno. She had the nerve to ask to talk to her friend. The first two phone calls were taken by Marie. The housekeeper repeated what Crafts told her, Helle was flying again. This seemed very odd to Rita since it was only Thursday morning and regulations required a 48 hour stand-down between flights. Rita voiced her fears to Marie that Helle was missing. Echoing in the back of the flight attendant's mind was her friend's statement, "If something happens to me, don't be-

lieve it was accidental." The housekeeper was adamant, Helle was not missing. Richard called Rita around 3 p.m. to tell her that his wife called from London and was en route to Denmark to visit her seriously ill mother, Lis Nielsen, in the hospital.

The news of Helle's mother's illness came as a surprise to Rita. Helle had called her mother four days ago and everything was fine. Rita asked Crafts to call Pan Am and request emergency leave for his wife. He declined, asking Rita to do it for him. Rita next requested Lis Nielsen's phone number. Richard gave her a number he claimed was Mrs. Nielsen's. It later proved to be false.

What Rita could not have known was that Crafts had called her from Danbury, after he picked up and hitched the all important woodchipper to the rented U-Haul. Driving a U-Haul with a woodchipper attached was tough going on the slush and ice covered roads. For all of the pilot's flying skills, he could not make time getting back to Newtown. He did not go home, for none of his neighbors ever reported seeing the U-Haul. It is thought that he took the woodchipper to his Currituck Road property.

Crafts claimed that he went to the police station for training exercises that evening, but discovered that they were cancelled. He further claimed to have stayed in a diner, drinking coffee, from 6 p.m. to 10 p.m., waiting for his shift to begin.

However, at 7 p.m., there was a mysterious man seen on the Silver Bridge. He was wearing a green poncho and wide brimmed Smoky the Bear hat, the same type of head gear worn by the police. The night was wet and nasty. Yet this unknown person was seen by Joe Williams grinding wood chips into the Housatonic River. It was not the smaller type that most people used, but an industrial strength woodchipper. Two observations made the whole scene stand out in Joe Williams' memory. One was the U-Haul used to tow the woodchipper. Not many people would do something like that in that part of the country. The other item that held Williams' attention was the clod on the bridge. He was polluting the river. Williams was a fisherman. He considered any pollution of the Housatonic a personal affront.

Crafts was seen several times that evening and early morning dragging the woodchipper around town. At one point Richard met one of his fellow officers at 4 a.m. His friend asked him why he needed such a powerful woodchipper. The part-time Newtown policeman answered the question with one word, "limbs."

It is now assumed that Crafts chain sawed his wife's body into chipper-sized pieces between 6 p.m. and 6:30 p.m. on his Currituck property. He must have laid out plastic drop cloths to catch any small

Murder is more likely to be committed by someone the victim knows,
rather than a stranger.

pieces. That night many of his neighbors were out cutting tree limbs broken by the snowstorm. One more chain saw buzzing away in the night would not have seemed unusual. Afterwards Richard bagged the body and drop cloths into six or seven plastic lawn bags. Crafts must have loaded the U-Haul with wood from the Currituck lot before he drove off for Silver Bridge.

Sometime near 3:30 a.m. Richard was seen with his woodchipper and U-Haul by Joe Hine, a road worker, on River Road. Hine drove past the same spot two hours later and noticed that there were six small mounds of wood chips along the road. The curious road worker thought the whole episode was quite odd, and for that reason the woodchipper sighting stuck in his memory. Hine could not have suspected that Crafts was cleaning out the bloody remains of his wife from the woodchipper.

Wood chips have a way of multiplying, and at an unknown time Crafts cleaned the woodchipper yet again on his Currituck Road property. When he was finished, he shoveled the pile into the trunk of his Crown Victoria. Later, much to his dismay, he would find tiny remnants of his wife's flesh and blood clinging to the mat. He threw the mat away. Somehow he never got around to replacing it.

Fire was the only sure way Richard knew to dispose of Helle's traveling bags, passport and personal effects. Crafts used the fireplace not for warmth but as an incinerator. Wearing the asbestos gloves he recently purchased, Crafts sifted through the ashes until he was certain that only ciders remained of Helle's belongings.

One item remained to tie everything in a neat package. Crafts had to drive the Tercel to Kennedy Airport. How this was accomplished was never discovered. He had to have some way of getting back to a second auto and drive home. It has been theorized that he used the Crown Victoria to tow it near the airport and walked back to his car afterward. Yet on November 22 Rita saw Helle's car parked in the Pan Am parking lot. Richard had solved this tough logistical problem.

Perfect murders are those that leave no clues and a lot of unanswerable questions. If Helle was not as popular as she was, she would not have had so many good friends. If she hadn't had so may good friends, they would not have pushed so hard to have her murder solved. If the murder hadn't been solved, Crafts would have committed the perfect crime. In the beginning, it looked as if he did.

Rita Buonanno began the process of bringing Richard to justice by simply calling Helle's mother. She quickly discovered that Crafts gave her the wrong number. Rita began discussing this strange turn of events with other flight attendants and mutual friends. The most worrisome aspect of Helle's disappearance was the lack of phone calls from her. Not only did she neglect to call her husband, or so he claimed, she did not even call her friends or ask for an emergency leave from Pan Am. This was totally out of character for the very responsible Helle, no matter what the circumstances.

Shortly before Thanksgiving Rita talked to the Crafts' housekeeper and received a mixed bag of information. On one hand Helle's suitcase was missing, which would have been normal if she was away from home. In addition, on the night of the snowstorm, Marie did not hear or see anything unusual. On the more ominous side of the ledger, the housekeeper reported seeing a large, dark brown blotch on the bedroom rug the next day. The bedroom rug along with the rugs from the children's rooms had suddenly disappeared two days later. Also missing was Helle's list of personal phone numbers from the kitchen cabinet. But most alarming of all was the fact that suddenly Marie's address book with a list of Helle's emergency phones had also vanished.

Thanksgiving had provided Rita a brief respite from the growing anxiety over the fate of her friend. When the holiday was over the dread returned. Several times during the last two weeks of November Rita, along with Helle's friends, Lee Ficheroulle, Jette Rompe and David Long, had contacted Crafts. Each of them found Richard's responses to their queries quite bizarre. He claimed ignorance of the location of the Pan Am parking lot, even though it was next to the one he used at Eastern. He further claimed that Helle's mother was sick and lying about her health. When this statement was disputed, Crafts asserted that since none of Helle's friends spoke Danish they had misunderstood her mother. When he was told that a Swede had talked to Lis Nielsen, and Swedes and Danes can understand each other very well, Richard said that Helle's mother was mentally ill. The final straw came at the end of November when Crafts stated that his wife was vacationing at Club Med in the Canary Islands. Helle's friends had heard enough from Mr. Crafts. It was time for action.

At 9 a.m., on December 1, Dianne Andersen received three phone calls from Helle's friends. Andersen agreed that Mrs. Crafts' disappearance sounded suspicious, especially in light of what Andersen knew about Helle. Helle was not the kind of woman who could be absent for such an extended period of time without contacting her children. Andersen called her private investigator friend, Keith Mayo. Mayo remembered the surveillance of Crafts that he had performed for Helle two months earlier, and horrible thought came to mind. His photos might have contributed to the woman's demise.

Mayo spent a whole day trying to convince the various Connecticut law enforcement agencies that Helle's disappearance was worthy of their time and should be investigated. His first call was to the Newtown Police Department. They were less than enthusiastic about examining the possibility that Helle's disappearance was a missing person case, let alone a murder. Crafts was one of their own, even if he was only part-timer.

Another reason for the local law enforcement reticence was the 72-year-old Newtown police chief, Lou Marchese. He had seen it all and no one was going tell him how to run his department. Marchese scheduled Mayo's meeting with one of his detectives at 4:30 in the afternoon. Both Mayo and Andersen met with assistant prosecutor Robert Brunetti at the Danbury Courthouse. He offered his help, as much as he could, without injuring any department's professional pride. Brunetti pointed out that there were no official investigations of Helle's disappearance at the moment, and until there was, he lacked any basis to speed the process along.

Mayo briefly questioned the housekeeper at the police station around 12:30 p.m. She told him about the events of November 18 and 19. Upon hearing her story Mayo became convinced that some horrible crime had been committed. Later in the afternoon, after Helle's friends had given their statements, it became apparent to the private investigator that the Newtown Police Department thought Mrs. Crafts' disappearance was a low priority use of their time.

It was apparent to rookie Patrolman Henry Stormer, after taking Marie Thomas' and Rita Buonanno's statements, that Mrs. Crafts was murdered by her husband. But he was in the minority of those who thought so at the Newtown Police Department, and he kept quiet about his suspicions.

The next day Richard Crafts was called into the station house for questioning. The detectives asked him why he took so long to report his wife missing. Crafts replied that she had gone away for extended periods before. What he really meant to say was that when Helle was working and away from home, it was sometimes for as long as a week. When asked where she might be, Crafts replied either vacationing at Club Med in the Canary Islands, or visiting her friend in Florida, or she might have run off with an Oriental lover.

Crafts signed a statement indicating that his wife left home early in the morning of November 19 and he had not seen her since. Since this statement was legally a missing persons report, the Newtown Police Department could put their investigative wheels in motion. Before he left the station, the detectives asked Crafts if he would take a lie detector test. He eagerly agreed. Richard's enthusiasm for the test made the detectives suspicious.

During the next few days Mayo kept stirring things up at the state prosecutor's office in Danbury. He was going to keep this case alive and he was going to use any method he thought would be effective. He called up an acquaintance, the editor of the Danbury *News Times*, and gave him the developing story. Mayo did this in a manner as to imply that this might be the local murder of the decade, but he cautioned, discretion was definitely required. The editor put Patrick O'Neil, his most energetic reporter, on the story.

When the private investigator learned that Crafts was willing to take a lie detector test, he was hopeful. When he further learned that Richard claimed his wife ran off with an Oriental gentleman from Westchester, he thought the police had caught Crafts in a big lie and was happy. But when he was told that Crafts passed the test, he was incredulous.

Lie detector tests (polygraphs) are not foolproof. If a guilty subject knows what he is doing, he can pass the test. One obvious method is to use emotion suppressing drugs, but these can be detected with blood or urine tests. Another is to take a drug whose side effects will flatten emotional response. Beta blocking agents, drugs used in the treatment of high blood pressure and heart disease, will do this. There is another way to foil a lie detector test. An acquaintance of Mayo's suggested that Crafts may have learned the CIA technique of using self-inflicted pain to throw off the questions used to determine the subject's normal base line.

It's a very simple procedure. The subject secretly causes himself pain when answering all innocuous questions. These queries are asked to establish the subject's basic response. This can be accomplished by biting one's tongue, biting on a toothpick wedged into a gum or pressing a toe on a thumbtack hidden in a shoe. When a loaded question is asked, there is no self-inflected pain. All the responses would appear to have the same contours on the graph. Mayo surmised that Crafts did something such as this.

There is another way to fool a lie detector, and Lt. DeJoseph suspected that Crafts was the kind of guy who could pull it off. Richard may have been the kind of cool customer who did not need any special preparation. This kind of individual can lie without showing any fluctuations in his breathing, heart rate, blood pressure and sweat. This kind of person, for whatever reason, does not fear being discovered.

Sometimes the polygraph cannot measure certain reactions. About three percent of the population can

Lie detectors have come a long way since this 1930s model, but the
results are still subject to dispute and controversy. A clever subject
can manipulate responses to fool the machine.

give those types of responses that cannot be accurately analyzed. When Richard first joined the Newtown police force he took a lie detector test. His reactions on the graph came out unusually flat. The examiner who gave that test had only seen one other result like that in his whole career. However Crafts accomplished it was immaterial. Crafts passing the lie detector test kept the investigation of Helle's disappearance classified as a missing persons case.

David Rogers felt that Crafts killed Helle, even if Rogers' wife did not. Later he would develop his own theory on how his brother-in-law passed the lie detector test. He reasoned that Crafts could not have been emotionally influenced by guilt since he believed no one would ever find the body.

DeJoseph and the other Newtown policemen, assigned to what was only a missing persons case, tried other avenues of investigation. They began to look at Crafts' credit card purchases. In addition they obtained a list of contents from the safe deposit box Helle shared with Rita. To their surprise all the jewelry that Crafts claimed his wife took with her was on the list.

At the same time Keith Mayo convinced Dianne Andersen and Helle's friends to hire him. Once the formalities were out of the way, Mayo ascertained from the group that no one had ever heard of the Oriental lover that Crafts claimed his wife had been seeing. To no one's surprise further inquiry by the private investigator concluded the story was a figment of Richard's imagination.

Helle's Tercel had top priority. But no matter what Mayo did he could not obtain permission from Pan Am to search the car, nor could he convince the Newtown Police to do the same. In the end searching the car would prove immaterial to the case.

On December 10 Mayo talked with Marie Thomas again. She told him that a few days after Helle's disappearance Crafts said he was glad she was out of his life. But what really interested Mayo was the missing stained rug from the master bedroom. It had a large dark patch on it and Crafts tried to clean it himself. The housekeeper said that Richard had gotten rid of the rug because it smelled of kerosene. This struck Mayo as odd since kerosene odor does not last long. Kerosene has been used as a traditional spot remover for exactly that reason. She also mentioned other rugs were removed from the house and replaced with new ones. This was the first he had heard about the rugs and he was deeply interested.

In a conversation with Brunetti, Mayo learned some misinformation that started a wild goose chase for the missing Crafts' rug. Brunetti, who confused two stories and made them one, told Mayo that

Crafts was seen acting strangely in the Southbury garbage dump. The original stories were of Richard acting strangely at his other part-time job as a construction security guard, and the Southbury police obtaining the key for the garbage station's dumpster. But once the private investigator heard the confused version it was off to the races. And the race would take him clear across the state.

The private investigator made inquiries as to where the Southbury garbage was sent, since the small town lacked facilities to handle the refuse on its own. It turned out that the only large Connecticut landfill that accepted small town debris was near the Rhode Island boarder. When Mayo arrived at the site he discovered that one of the landfill operators had found a bloody bra in the Southbury refuse. The investigator's euphoria was short lived when he further learned that the operator threw it back. But Mayo was still in luck, due to heavy rains in the past few days, some 20 odd tons of Southbury garbage was still in one pile. Of course most people would find the idea of searching through 20 tons of garbage anything but lucky.

Using most of his retainer money, Mayo hired a crew and a backhoe to sift through the Southbury debris. Several days later they found some rugs. At first the searchers thought they had the wrong ones because the colors weren't right. When the internal fibers were examined, it became apparent that the rugs were discolored due to exposure to the elements. On December 17 Mayo sent the rugs to the Eastern District Major Crime Squad. They would later conclude that the rug samples were not from the Crafts' bedroom. But it really did not matter, because the rugs resulted in bringing the state police into the case.

"Police Seek Missing Newtown Woman," the headline screamed, as the Danbury *News Times* published Patrick O'Neil's story on Helle's disappearance. The effect of this news story was to send Mayo into a panic. He was afraid that Marie Thomas' life would now be in danger. He called Andersen and she convinced States Attorney Walter Flanagan to interview Thomas the next day. Thomas was sent to one of Mayo's clients for the evening. What happened next was comparable to two parents battling over the custody of a child. In this situation it was two police departments fighting for jurisdiction in the Crafts' case.

From all outward appearances the Newtown Police Department was not interested in the Crafts' case. But inside the station house there was a lot of speculation as to what really happened to Helle. Much of the confusion as to their intent had to do with an old dispute between the local police departments, the state police and the states attorney's office. The ill will began with a 1973 murder case when it was discovered that the police departments involved obtained a confession under dubious circumstances. Later the state police department used undue influence with the state's attorney to get a conviction. A 1976 hearing found that many of these charges were true, the conviction was overturned, and in the aftermath of these findings the Eastern and Western Major Crime Squads were created as the investigative arms of the states' attorney office under the command of the state police.

When someone like Lou Marchese enters into the existing crime solving equation, you get chaos. Marchese was not one to kowtow to the Western District Major Crime Squad. He had been around too long and seen too many new units come and go. For the old police chief this particular case was comparable to having a mosquito bite on a big toe. It constantly reminds the bitten individual it is there, it won't go away and there is very little that one can do about it in public. Marchese felt trapped by the big guys. They had the budget, they had the resources and they felt that Crafts had killed Helle. Some of his own detectives had come to the same conclusion. The police chief began to think of the case as a challenge to his department and his local authority.

Many time-consuming meetings occurred between members of the Newtown Police Department and Western District Major Crime Squad. Some conferences were in person, some were on the telephone and some were a combination of both. The politics of the matter was the politics of toe stepping, and everyone ended up walking around with a slight limp. The upshot of all this talk was Marchese's decision to solve the case on his own, much to the annoyance of the Western District Major Crime Squad. However, working at cross purposes, both police forces discovered some important clues.

The Newtown police discovered that Helle had type O-positive blood. They also obtained copies of her dental records. DeJoseph surveyed the Currituck Road property and noticed a pile of wood chips camouflaged by some branches. This oddity had no meaning to the Newtown detective at the time. As a matter of routine procedure it was discovered that Crafts had a habit of using credit cards for all his purchases. The Newtown police were told by one of Helle's friends that Richard's sister had seen some brownish spots staining Crafts' mattress. This bit of information made Richard's December 19 purchase of a new set of bedding, found on another charge slip, all the more interesting.

The charge card trail led straight to the most interesting discovery of all, the woodchipper. When Newtown detectives came across the charge slip itemizing the rental at Darien Rentals from November 18-21, there was no one in the station house who wasn't at least a little shocked. There was also no one in the Newtown Police Department who didn't believe that Crafts had killed his wife and ground her up into little pieces.

The investigators from the Western District Crime Squad had less initial success. All they had to go on were the statements from Helle's friends, Marie Thomas' tape recorded accounts of the days surrounding the disappearance, Mayo's photos and description of the night Crafts spent with Nancy Dodd, Richard's inconsistencies with his own statements and with the statements of Helle's friends.

The state police also knew that the Newtown Police Department was withholding valuable clues, and obstructing justice of a matter with jurisdiction. And yet with so little evidence the state police gambled by taking a crucial step, they got a search warrant.

The state police were afraid the judge would refuse the warrant on the grounds that they lacked probable cause. On Christmas Eve Judge Frank McDonald reviewed facts as stated in the search warrant and commented on their flimsy nature. Thinking about the matter for a moment he said, "This is one of those cases where you are damned if you do and damned if you don't." And perhaps as a gesture of Christmas good will he signed the warrant.

On the day after Christmas the state police moved with the speed of an army in a Latin American takeover. In the morning the Western District Major Crime Squad notified the Newtown Police Department they were kicked off the case. Spitefully Police Chief Lou Marchese told them they were making a big mistake. When the detectives at the station house heard the news they were demoralized. They were angry, feeling their competence as policemen was being questioned. As far as the state police were concerned, it was.

At about 4 p.m. a small company of state police legally invaded Crafts' home. As stated in the search warrant, they were allowed to examine everything and seize anything that might pertain to the case. Once inside the police found the house was a mess. It was evident that Helle was responsible for the orderliness of the Craft domicile; during her prolonged absence chaos crept in. Richard was away, so the search went on unhindered. One of the unexpected finds was that the padding under the new rug was two-thirds removed. Was the old padding stained with blood that had seeped through the overlaying rug?

After photographing the location of all the items in the master bedroom and living room, the state police seized some of Helle's belongings for later examination. They also seized Crafts' Ford Crown Victoria along with his small arsenal of bullets and guns. He had enough firepower to make a terrorist gang very happy. Included in his armaments' collection were two live hand grenades that had to be disarmed by experts.

It was now time for Henry Lee, the state police's forensic expert, to examine the bedroom. His preliminary testing of the smears on the mattress indicated they were positive for blood, so were some of the washcloths and towels in the bathroom. From the angle and shape of the blood spots on the mattress, Lee concluded that Helle was not lying down when she was attacked. Anything more that could be learned from the items the state police seized would have to wait until Lee had time to thoroughly examine everything.

Waiting is not something the Western District Major Crime Squad investigators like to do. So they canvassed the area for possible witnesses to anything unusual on the nights in question. They found a Southbury police officer who remembered seeing Crafts towing a woodchipper around town while he was on duty. From the same officer the detective learned that road worker, Joe Hine, had noticed a woodchipper parked on River Road after midnight.

The mention of a woodchipper brought a recent crime to a Western District Major Crime Squad investigator's mind. About a year before a young man was convicted of putting a German shepherd dog through a woodchipper because the dog barked to much. This raised the question, "Did Crafts grind up his wife because she wanted a divorce?"

What was just an ugly speculation began to grow into an uglier reality. The state police invited Henry Stormer to their Troop A building for a professional chat. Henry was still upset about the way the Western District Major Crime Squad had treated the Newtown Police Department. But there was such a thing as professional courtesy and besides his co-worker, Detective DeJoseph, thought a talk with the state police might be beneficial in the long run for the Newtown Police Department.

Stormer confirmed that Crafts had rented the industrial strength woodchipper for the time period in question. An electric shock went through the Western District Major Crime Squad detectives as they realized this was no ordinary crime. They quickly moved to plug any leaks of their discovery. If such sensational news was prematurely released it would warn Crafts that they were on to him and subsequently damage their case.

Joseph Hine was a crucial witness. He had seen a man on River Road, dressed in a trooper's orange poncho, standing next to a U-Haul with a woodchipper attached. As he approached another car came down the road from the opposite direction. The man then motioned him by as a state trooper might do. This occurred between 3:30 and 4 a.m. It was a very weird sight in the middle of a stormy night. Later he saw the same truck and woodchipper on the Silver Bridge. In the early morning light he rode back down River Road and noticed a half a dozen wood chip piles on the side of the road. Even the most blasé detectives were dumbfounded at the implications of Hine's story.

Hine led the detectives to the place where he had noticed the wood chips on River Road. Since he had first seen the pile of chips, almost a month and half ago, Hine observed that someone had flattened the piles with some kind of a hand tool, such as a shovel. Mixed in a few of the piles was a blue cloth-like substance. A brief search of the surrounding area yielded evidential pay dirt, an American Cancer Society envelope addressed to Helle Crafts!

At 1 p.m., on December 27, more evidence was gathered in the River Road area of Newtown. A small group of police officers searched as quietly as possible, so as not to give any warning to Crafts that they were actively investigating the murder of Helle and not her disappearance. They picked up everything that might have belonged to or might have been part of Helle Crafts. Some of the objects included strands of blond hair, possible bone fragments and labels for a brand of vitamins that Helle sold in her spare time.

After the state police sifted through 30 plus bags of debris, only a tiny pile of evidence remained. It was a grisly pile consisting of bone fragments identified as belonging to the interior of a human skull, some tiny chopped up strands of blond hair and one dented dental crown. The crown was a very important find since it would be found to match up with Helle's dental records.

On January 2 as soon all the New Years' celebrations were over, Dr. Lee examined the trunk of the Ford Crown Victoria. His curiosity was aroused because he thought it was odd for a trunk to be missing its mat. He found minute human fragments clinging to the walls. These included bone, hair and flesh. There were also some tiny bits of unexplained shredded blue material. At the trial it was learned the blue material probably came from Helle's shredded nightgown.

On January 6 detectives from the the Western District Major Crime Squad conducted an interview with Richard Crafts. Crafts was told that Helle's disappearance was still under investigation. Unknown to the police, Crafts already knew from his brother-in-law's discussion with some of the Newtown police that the detectives had uncovered his woodchipper rental at the time of Helle's disappearance.

It was a rambling and mumbling three hours. Crafts made a few strange slips. For example, when he was asked what he told his children about their mother being gone for so long he replied, "The police are looking for him," quickly adding, "for Mommy." Crafts came across as quite emotionless throughout the interview, except when he mentioned his children, then he actually cried. His coldness about his wife's disappearance and his complete lack of interest in her whereabouts left the the detectives with the feeling they were talking to a man who had murdered his wife.

Working on a hunch that perhaps Crafts had thrown more than woodchipping debris from the Silver Bridge, the state police sent divers into the swift icy waters of the Housatonic to look for clues on January 7. It was dangerous work but after a few hours of searching it paid off. The divers recovered a chain saw housing and chain. It was immediately noticed that the housing had its serial number filed off. Two days later they found the chain saw blade partially buried in the sandy river bottom.

Work continued at the River Road site under a large tent. The tent served two purposes, it kept the searchers warm and kept their work from the prying eyes of the press. They worked at a meticulous pace, examining every piece of debris that looked as if it might have a bearing on the case. Several days later the state police had recovered a toe joint, a partial portion of a finger with the nail attached and a porcelain cap with fragments of a tooth and bone.

Not wanting to leave any possible clues unexamined, the Western District Major Crime Squad tracked down the U-Haul that Crafts used to lug the woodchipper around that fateful night and gave it a through going over. To no one's surprise they found some blue fibers, reddish stains, tiny bone fragments and blond hair.

It was now time to make a decision in the case. Was there enough evidence to convict Crafts? The state's medical examiner, H. Wayne Carver II, thought it could go one of two ways. If one looked at only the lie detector test and physical evidence collected so far, one might conclude that it was merely a case of improper disposal of a dead body. This crime was just a misdemeanor.

If one took into account the inconsistencies of Crafts' statements, coupled with the illogical disappearance of Helle Crafts from a regular and responsible lifestyle, one could only come to the conclusion that Richard Crafts had murdered his wife. It was a case of homicide.

Arresting Richard Crafts was not a cut and dry affair. Around 7 p.m. the radio announced that Crafts was about to be arrested for the murder of his wife. At the same time a police radio car was parked nearby watching the house. It wasn't until 11 p.m. that the arrest warrant was ready. During that time Richard's sister, Karen Rogers, went to her brother's house and asked the patrol car to notify her if the worst happened and she would take care of the children. This was highly unlikely in the best of circumstances since she was the suspect's sister and might conceivably be involved in the case.

A few minutes after the arrest warrant was signed, the state police called Crafts on the telephone. They asked him to come outside and someone would be there to arrest him. Richard replied, "I'm tired, I'll take care of it in the morning." When he was told that this was an order, not a request, he hung up.

Perhaps Crafts could not believe this was happening to him. Some murderers think they will never be caught. Perhaps he really wanted his brother-in-law to take his children. In response to Richard's hurried phone call, David Rogers agreed to get to the house as quickly as possible and take the Craft children. He arrived too late.

At first the state police thought they had overlooked some of Richard's impressive arsenal and Crafts was thinking of shooting it out with them with whatever guns, rifles or grenades remained. They called him on the telephone again and pointed out that if he waited until morning he would have a hoard of news people gathered around, to say nothing of flying about the house in helicopters. This would certainly upset his children. Crafts promised to give himself up at a quarter past midnight. He was waiting for David. The police did not know this and prepared for the worst. A sharpshooter armed with a scoped rifle was hidden nearby with a full view of the house. If Crafts was going to shoot it out they were prepared to kill him as quickly as possible.

The deadline came and went and still no Richard Crafts. The police telephoned again and told him to keep his end of the bargain. He said he was saying good-bye to his children. Twenty minutes later David Rogers did not show up and Richard Crafts emerged from his house. He was quickly arrested. It was all over.

There were two trials. The first one ended in a

hung jury. It was not as bad as it sounds. There was only one hold out, but that was all that was needed. In November 1989 a second jury found Richard Crafts guilty in the murder of his wife Helle.

At the sentencing, his sister, Karen Rogers, complained that her brother had shown no remorse. Until his arrest she was his staunchest supporter. After two trials and several long conversations with her brother, she told Superior Court Judge Martin L. Nigro, "I am concerned that Mr. Crafts has not publicly nor privately demonstrated any remorse for the murder of his wife. I believe he has paid lip service only to the concerns of the children."

In his defense, Crafts said before he was sentenced, "A great deal has been said about my apparent lack of emotion: 'He has ice water in his veins.' I have feelings like everyone else." On January 8, 1990, the judge sentenced Richard Crafts to 50 years in prison. David and Karen Rogers gained custody of the Crafts' three children.

Index

Photo Credits

All photographs have been supplied by Bettman Archive, the Library of Congress, Stephen McKenna and the author. All the color photographs were taken especially for this book.